AF323231

Coriolanus

Recent Titles in
Greenwood Guides to Shakespeare

Macbeth: A Guide to the Play
H. R. Coursen

Hamlet: A Guide to the Play
W. Thomas MacCary

Julius Caesar: A Guide to the Play
Jo McMurtry

Romeo and Juliet: A Guide to the Play
Jay L. Halio

Othello: A Guide to the Play
Joan Lord Hall

The Tempest: A Guide to the Play
H. R. Coursen

King Lear: A Guide to the Play
Jay L. Halio

Love's Labour's Lost: A Guide to the Play
John S. Pendergast

Antony and Cleopatra: A Guide to the Play
Joan Lord Hall

As You Like It: A Guide to the Play
Steven J. Lynch

The Merchant of Venice: A Guide to the Play
Vicki K. Janik

A Midsummer Night's Dream: A Guide to the Play
Jay L. Halio

CORIOLANUS

A Guide to the Play

MARY STEIBLE

Greenwood Guides to Shakespeare

GREENWOOD PRESS
Westport, Connecticut • London

Library of Congress Cataloging-in-Publication Data

Steible, Mary.
Coriolanus : a guide to the play / Mary Steible.
p. cm.—(Greenwood guides to Shakespeare)
Includes bibliographical references and index.
ISBN 0–313–32962–1 (alk. paper)
1. Shakespeare, William, 1564–1616. Coriolanus. 2. Coriolanus, Cnaeus Marcius—In literature. 3. Generals in literature. 4. Rome—In literature. I. Title. II. Series.
PR2805.S74 2004
822.3'3—dc22 2004056068

British Library Cataloguing in Publication Data is available.

Library of Congress Catalog Card Number: 2004056068
ISBN: 0–313–32962–1

First published in 2004

Greenwood Press, 88 Post Road West, Westport, CT 06881
An imprint of Greenwood Publishing Group, Inc.
www.greenwood.com

Printed in the United States of America

The paper used in this book complies with the Permanent Paper Standard issued by the National Information Standards Organization (Z39.48-1984).

10 9 8 7 6 5 4 3 2 1

CONTENTS

PREFACE

> . . . no one has ever excelled, in art of any kind, over the sheer concentrated immensity, the intellectual and emotional achievement, of this poet's late tragedies.[1]

The last of Shakespeare's "late" tragedies, *The Tragedy of Coriolanus* (1608–1610) most likely followed the drafting of *Antony and Cleopatra* (1607–1608), with *Timon of Athens* being written sometime during the same period.[2] These three tragedies share a common source, Thomas North's translation of Plutarch's *Lives of Famous Greeks and Romans.*[3] Of the three, *Antony and Cleopatra* and *Coriolanus* are a return to the Roman-themed tragedy that Shakespeare introduced in the earliest of his tragedies, *Titus Andronicus* (1590), and a decade later in *Julius Caesar* (1599).

Coriolanus may be the first dramatic treatment of Caius Martius Coriolanus for the English stage.[4] Martius[5] remained a popular figure on post-Restoration stages in England, and then America, through the early twentieth century. Why Shakespeare turns to Caius Martius, a figure not quite as popular as Julius Caesar or Marcus Antony, as a subject for his last tragedy is not known. Post-Restoration dramatists who adapted Shakespeare's *Coriolanus* make their purposes clear: Martius's story represents the conflict between upper and lower ranks of society, and as changes in societal make-up challenged the nature of rank, and thus civil and natural rights, dramatists exploited the old tale from Plutarch and other classical Roman authors to show their support of the rulers or the ruled.

Living in a culture that designated people as belonging to lower and higher ranks or orders, Shakespeare perhaps found the conflicts between the various groups (today referred to as "class conflicts") topical during a period of English history in which economic stresses pitted commoner against monarchical authority. Perhaps Shakespeare was intrigued by the way an individual, Caius Martius, asserted himself so strongly against societal and political change that he found himself alienated from the culture that nourished him. Whatever the case, Shakespeare's last tragedy is a triumphant end to his tragic "phase" and is as relevant to today's audiences as to audiences in 1608. Like Shakespeare, we ponder the nature of economic structures, social values, public policies, and the place of the individual in a social order. The matchless dramatic skill with which Shakespeare presents myriad personal and social concerns through character, verse, and plot in a tragic form relays a powerful statement on the human condition in a complex world. The individual Roman and the Romans are represented as being dependent on each other to the extent that all individuals' actions, not just those of the great and powerful, are shown to have consequences and effects on a community. The relationship between action and consequence is seen in Martius, who is pure tragic character. An extraordinary Roman warrior, devoted husband, and obedient son, Caius Martius is one of the most virtuous and noble of Shakespeare's heroes; on the other hand, he is ill-mannered, unable to govern his temper or his tongue once angered. That tragic consequences will follow is made clear by the fear, anxiety, and tension that Martius creates within the Roman community. In *Coriolanus*, Martius is most angered by the plebeians' rights to a voice in government. His caustic tirades toward them do more than lead to his banishment from Rome; they reveal the deeply riven class divide, not to mention the hypocrisy of Roman ideals of citizenship in an increasingly complex city or *urbs*.[6]

This study of *Coriolanus* begins with its textual history. The play text, first printed in the 1623 *Folio* edition of Shakespeare's works,[7] shows how artfully Shakespeare integrated stage movement and stage sounds with lines of verse and prose. Textual scholars have made a good case that the *Folio* text is a copy from Shakespeare's own hand. Despite some textual corruptions that may or may not have been Shakespeare's, the greater part of the text we read today can be studied as an example of Shakespeare's mature work, and it is the work of a playwright who is seasoned in writing, staging, and acting plays. Because there is no record of *Coriolanus* being staged during Shakespeare's lifetime, textual scholars dating the play have had to rely on topical data, such as contemporary events, and the dating of works of other writers to which Shakespeare may allude. Some of the topical data both strengthen and weaken critical arguments about Shakespeare's interest in politics, economics, or justice, which we will see in Chapters 4 and 5.

The relationship between Shakespeare's primary source for the play, contemporary events, and the theatrical context is discussed in Chapter 2. First, though, each of these elements is discussed as a springboard for a number of themes and critical approaches. The Roman hero in *Coriolanus* is not only the subject of one of Plutarch's moral narratives but also the product of an evolving cultural practice: the writing and staging of tragedies for public entertainment. During the nascence and development of the early modern stage in England, between the opening of the Theater in 1576 until Shakespeare's retirement from the stage, other poets[8] drew on Roman historical narratives and biographies for tragic subjects. At the same time, the genre of tragedy was evolving out of several antecedent traditions: classical,[9] English medieval, and sixteenth-century tragic narrative.

Two monarchs, Elizabeth I and James I, sat on the throne of England during this period. Their attitudes toward patronage, licensing, and censorship played critical roles in the development of the stage. Talents of actors and stage practices, too, figured in the design of a Roman tragic character. From these known cultural practices, we can situate *Coriolanus* in a mature position both in Shakespeare's own canon and in early English theater. In the backdrop of the development of staging Roman tragic heroes is the sociopolitical climate of the period in which Shakespeare wrote. The institutions that dominated life in precapitalist England, such as government and religion, were negotiated by individuals in a number of ways, through families, the educational system, or collectively popular traditions from the Anglo past. Meanwhile, plagues and harvest failures affected labor and economics. The closing of the stages during plagues, for instance, put actors and stage managers out of work in the city, and they sought work in the rural areas of England. Harvest failures caused loss of earnings, not to mention the loss of nourishment for the most vulnerable. Enclosure laws led to the Midlands Insurrection of 1607, an event which may have been influential in the writing of *Coriolanus*.

Today *Coriolanus* may not be one of Shakespeare's most popular or well-known tragedies or plays, despite its successes on the eighteenth- and nineteenth-century stage as shown in Chapter 6 of this guide, but it is a provocative play. Twentieth-century critics and audiences alike have responded to the play in a number of ways. One critic suggested that

Coriolanus was an unpopular play because audiences and readers in democratic societies could not enjoy a play that presented the "people" in such an indecorous light, as if it were presumed the people had to be portrayed as brutish.[10] In one instance, the hero, the conservative, patrician Martius, was perceived to be aligned with Fascists and Communists, who "rioted" a Paris production in the 1930s because they felt the play was "propaganda directed at them."[11] It is unfortunate that *Coriolanus* has been judged and censured for its political content when, indeed, it is superb tragic theater. Thus, in Chapter 3, the play is considered as a whole—not just as a play about a conflict between patricians and plebeians, but as a play about a tragic subject who fails to see the conflict that he harbors within himself. Derek Traversi sees these conflicts as related to one another, and, indeed, inseparable.[12] The great strength of Caius Martius puts him in the position of being demi-godlike, a great product of Roman military training, yet at the same time, this godlike military machine bullies the plebeians—Romans—the very people his training has prepared him to protect. His duty to the state, to the family, and to the gods he follows as a script, but his limited view of service to the state creates tension within himself and those around him. From the opening of the play until the end, Caius Martius is a conflicted man, a sound and a fury, never at peace with himself or with his social order.

Whereas Chapter 3 considers the play as a whole, Chapter 4 takes up some of the play's themes—the mother/son relationship, the class conflict, the individual and society, political idealism, social chaos. In *Coriolanus*, these themes are tightly interwoven, so that each theme creates the whole we see in Chapter 3. In relief, however, the themes show us how little or how much Volumnia dominates Martius's life, or how unstable Martius's Rome is in the early years of the struggling Roman republic. Most of these themes can be found in Shakespeare's other plays, but those specific to the setting of Rome may be the most meaningful. Shakespeare returns to the Roman setting throughout his career. Shakespeare's Roman characters, to be sure, are his own interpretation as he came to know them through his culture and its educational system. Still, the Roman plays and their characters make up a body of their own, and in *Coriolanus*, we see Shakespeare comfortably working with familiar ideas in a familiar setting.

Critical approaches to *Coriolanus*, the subject of Chapter 5, are varied, and as is so often the case, they tell us mostly about the critics and what was popular in critical activity during their lifetimes. Neoclassicists of the seventeenth century have interpreted Shakespeare according to their literary taste and style; cultural critics of the twenty-first century have focused on the cultural context of the plays. *Coriolanus* has been particularly interesting to critics of genre, as well as to political, psychoanalytical, and historical critics. A. C. Bradley and Maynard Mack consider Shakespeare's patterns of construction in plot and character in their treatments of the tragedies that provide springboards for discussion and reflection. The relationship between Volumnia and Martius has attracted feminist critics, who have drawn illuminating parallels between the play's focus on famine, the belly, and hunger and feeding mothers. Janet Adelman's *Suffocating Mothers* is a fascinating interrogation of the play's language of starvation and hunger, self-imposed and otherwise, and its relationship to the hero's psychological and emotional growth. New historicist and cultural materialist critics have performed fair service to the text by treating the political troubles represented in the play from the standpoint of genre, Jacobean politics, theatrical conventions, Shakespeare's understanding of Roman culture, or the social conditions and practices of seventeenth-century England. Leah S. Marcus's "*Coriolanus* and the Expansion of City Liberties," which relates Shakespeare's England and the burgeoning concept of civil liberties to *Coriolanus*, is one of the finest political readings of the play to date in its reflection on, rather than assumptions about, Shakespeare's political world. In both the theater and critical approaches to the text, Caius Martius Coriolanus has been perceived as "conservative" politically, to be sure, but whether or not conservative means "right" or "arrogant" or "oppressive" depends on the reader. Many choose to take political sides without considering that perhaps Shakespeare was exploring ideas about natural rights and civil rights too, not just making a statement on absolutist governments or republicanism and how they might work in his own culture.

Coriolanus in the theater, as Chapter 6 shows, begins its history in the Restoration, at which time it was adapted by Nahum Tate and entitled *The Ingratitude of a Commonwealth* (1682). As the title indicates, the play's political bent was toward the ruling class, not the people. Like most adaptations of Shakespeare, *The Ingratitude* freely borrowed lines and passages from Shakespeare's text but then rearranged, cut, or added text to suit theatrical and poetic fashions of the day. John Dennis similarly adapts *Coriolanus* in *The Invader of His Country* (1720). As the title suggests, the play supports rights for citizens against arrogant rulers. In 1749, James Thomson's blank-verse *Coriolanus* was staged. A more neoclassical-styled play than political statement, Thomson's version becomes a source for Thomas Sheridan's *The Roman Matron* (1754), a blend of Shakespeare and Thomson, with Sheridan playing the lead role beginning in December of that year. Earlier in November of 1754, David Garrick launched a "revival" of Shakespeare's *Coriolanus*, marking the start of Shakespeare's version being played regularly on the English stage, albeit in theatrical versions of the text, not the text that we read or are likely to see on an American or English stage. Through the mid-nineteenth century, Coriolanus remained a popular character for some of the finest talents of the time: Thomas Sheridan, Philip Kemble, William Macready, and others. Critical in Chapter Six are the ways in which actors and producers interpreted Shakespeare's text and how those texts then influenced the way that critics began treating the text in their studies.

I wish to thank George Butler for his thoughtful and encouraging readings of drafts of this guide. For supporting my trip to see the Royal Shakespeare Company perform *Coriolanus* in March 2003, I thank Associate Dean David Steinberg and Department of English Chair Charles Berger at Southern Illinois University Edwardsville.

NOTES

1. Park Honan, "The Tragic Sublime," in *Shakespeare: A Life* (Oxford: Oxford UP, 1998), p. 349.

2. The dates for Shakespeare's last three tragedies are not known; *Timon* might have been written after *Antony and Cleopatra* and before *Coriolanus*, according to the Arden Shakespeare *Coriolanus*, first prepared, introduced, and edited by W. J. Craig and R. H. Case. I cite this information from J. Philip Brockbank's edition *Coriolanus: The Arden Shakespeare* (London: Methuen, 1976) which he updated in 1975 (28). On the other hand, *The Riverside Shakespeare*, Ed. G. Blakemore Evans, offers proposed dates of composition as *Antony and Cleopatra* (1606–1607), *Coriolanus* (1607–1608), and *Timon of Athens* (1607–1608), in that order, the idea being forwarded in the *Riverside* that *Timon* had yet to be completed (86).

3. Plutarch's *Lives* was translated from Jacques Amyot's French translation of Plutarch's Greek in 1579. In 1589 and 1603, the second and third editions of North's Plutarch were published. According to M. W. MacCallum in *Shakespeare's Roman Plays and Their Background* (London: Macmillan, 1910; rpt. London: Macmillan, 1935), Shakespeare likely used the third edition for *Coriolanus*, although he was undoubtedly familiar with the earlier editions (151–52).

4. D. A. Traversi, *The Roman Plays* (Stanford, CA: Stanford UP, 1963), p. 208.

5. I use "Martius," rather than "Coriolanus," when referring to Shakespeare's hero.

6. Robert Miola, in *Shakespeare's Rome* (Cambridge, England: Cambridge

UP, 1983), uses the term *urbs* to describe the contested ground in *Coriolanus* (17). Although the term is not used in the play, it is the Latin term that Shakespeare would have known as meaning "city."

7. Also known as the *First Folio*, the 1623 collection of Shakespeare's plays was assembled and published by Shakespeare's fellow actors John Heminge and Henrie Condell seven years after Shakespeare's death.

8. Playwrights. Writers of plays were called poets in the youth of the English theater, reminds Honan, *Shakespeare: A Life*, p. 106.

9. The classical period or tradition refers to the writings, as well as other arts, of the early Greeks and Romans.

10. Albert H. Tolman, "The Structure of Shakespeare's Tragedies with Special Reference to Coriolanus," *Modern Language Notes* 37 (1922): 458. Tolman, writing in the 1920s, speaks about critics in the early twentieth century, after the first world war.

11. Stanley D. McKenzie, " 'Unshout the Noise That Banish'd Martius': Structural Paradox and Dissembling in Coriolanus," *Shakespeare Studies* 18 (1986): 189.

12. Traversi, *Roman Plays*, p. 13.

1

TEXTUAL HISTORY

The textual history of *Coriolanus* begins with the 1623 *First Folio*, in which it was first printed. No quarto printing is known to exist.[1] John Heminge and Henry Condell, fellow actors and friends of Shakespeare, were the publishers of the *Folio*, claiming to have collected and presented each play as Shakespeare "conceived them," not the way "injurious imposters" had presented them earlier.[2] Other copies of some of Shakespeare's plays were in circulation prior to 1623, and probably some copies in circulation, although not all, were considered unauthorized versions or, rather, versions that did not reflect the work as Shakespeare wrote it for the companies to whom he sold his plays, the Lord Chamberlain's or the King's Men.[3] No extant copy in quarto exists to suggest that *Coriolanus* was in circulation in any version but that owned by his theater company. Fourteen of the thirty-six plays that appear in the *Folio* were edited from "good" quartos.[4]

From evidence of writing and production practices of other dramatists of the period, we can surmise how *Coriolanus* came to be published. No one can say with surety when the play was written, if it were staged, or where it was to be staged. Whether audiences liked it or who played the role of Martius is also unknown. The same is true of *Antony and Cleopatra*, the play Shakespeare is thought to have written just before *Coriolanus*. Although we often read Shakespeare as a literary text today, we should keep in mind that Shakespeare's plays were written for dramatic production and thus were not prepared and published in the same way as a work written for a reading audience. What Shakespeare wrote in his "hand," or "autograph," was sold to his theater group, who then became the owners of his text.[5] Shakespeare's final manuscript draft of a play, called the "foul papers," was prepared by the playhouse prompter for the promptbook or by a scribe who wrote a "fair copy" for the prompter.[6] At some point in the history of a text, the text's copy that was sent to the printer could have been transmitted through several hands, a scribe's, prompter's, or compositor's.[7]

In the case of *Coriolanus*, it is believed that Shakespeare's autograph copy was used for the copy published in the *Folio*, not a promptbook or a transcript of that promptbook. Even though it has been argued to the contrary,[8] it appears likely the autograph copy went to the compositors. Spelling and lineation inconsistencies in the *Folio Coriolanus* show the involvement of several compositors, who had their own distinct setting practices or habits that they incorporated into their print, as is evidenced by other pages they prepared for the *Folio*.[9] Other inconsistencies appear to be Shakespeare's. Thus, about three hands were involved in the *Folio* copy of *Coriolanus*. Admittedly, the inconsistencies in the *Folio Coriolanus* for the average reader pose few problems. Knowing how the text was set and printed, however, is insightful, because it shows that any interpretation of the text that is forwarded today should still be checked against the original.[10]

Textual scholars have determined that the *Folio* was set by a number of compositors, who are referred to as A, B, C, D, and E. About half of the *Folio* tragedies were set from available printed quartos by Compositor E, who was only known to set type from printed copy. *Coriolanus* was never a printed quarto, so Compositor E has been ruled out as the person who set the text. Textual evidence suggests compositors A and B prepared *Coriolanus*, judging by spelling practices and other data.[11] In its original inception, the *Folio* had *Coriolanus* leading a group of twelve tragedies. Thus, *Coriolanus* is numbered pages 1–30 in the tragedies' section of the *Folio*. Each page is set with a center rule, which divides the two-column presentation of text. Box rules encase the title, *The Tragedy of Coriolanus*, with a handsome border above it, on the first page. Beneath the title, in separate box rules, is labeled the act and scene division, *Actus Primus. Scena Prima.* This is the only scene division mentioned, although the remaining four acts are labeled and set in box rules within the text. A running header in box rules, *The Tragedy of Coriolanus* and a page number, marks the top of each page. At the bottom of each page following the right column is a lead-in, or the first word or two of the text that will be found on the top left-hand column of the following page. Ending on page 30 close to the bottom of the page, the Latin *FINIS* closes the text. Besides the first page border, no other ornamentation is present.

The *First Folio* is the most authentic version of *Coriolanus*. Like the other plays in the *First Folio*, *Coriolanus* was transmitted to us through a series of editors beginning with Nicholas Rowe in 1709. Rowe's edition was based largely upon the 1685, or *Fourth Folio*.[12] This edition, like the two before it, showed no evidence of being an edited version of the original. It was simply the third reproduction of the original, and with every reproduction, errors and problems were introduced.[13] Rowe's octavo editions mark a number of "firsts": the first to have illustrations, to discontinue the *Folio* format (which was quite large and cumbersome), to add *dramatis personae* to some plays, to modernize spelling and punctuation, to divide plays into acts and scenes (where it had not been done), and to add locations.[14] Rowe is credited with being the first, too, to bring Shakespeare to a broad reading audience.[15]

After Rowe, Alexander Pope edited the *Folio* in 1725, making emendations to the text to suit eighteenth-century ideas of meter or grammar.[16] The changes, like those of Rowe's, were not grounded in scholarship[17] as much as they were in taste, and the result was later editors' having to restore some of the originally published passages to their original. In Pope's *Coriolanus*, for example, one significant change that he made was in the passage by Cominius on Martius's great strength to the senators and Menenius and others:

> As weeds before
> A vessel under sail, so men obeyed
> And fell below his stem.

"Weeds" was in the *Folio*, but later editions of *Folio*s changed "weeds" to "waves," and then Pope changed "stem" to "stern." "Weeds" should have no more been changed than "stem," but because of careless setting or an error by a printer, and in the case of Pope a desire to edit according to taste and sense, the original was lost. Both terms suit the context and quite adequately show the limpness of the enemy in the face of Martius's onslaught, as wet weeds before the stem or prow of a ship. It was not until Edmond Malone's 1790 edition that the text was corrected.[18]

Pope's alteration, although interesting, was arbitrary, and consequently made it his text rather than Shakespeare's. A habit among post-Restoration dramatists to "adapt" Shakespeare's plays might have led Rowe and Pope to view Shakespeare's text as one which needed correcting. The text of

Coriolanus was adapted by several post-Restoration dramatists, who argued their changes were necessary to improve what they felt were faults in Shakespeare's scripting.[19] That Rowe and Pope would modify Shakespeare's plays to align them with the literary conventions of the period is not unusual. After Rowe and Pope, Lewis Theobold (1733), Edward Capell (1768), and Edmond Malone (1790), notable eighteenth-century editors of the *Folio*, along with Samuel Johnson (1765), prepared editions of the *Folio* with another purpose in mind. Theobald's edition, in fact, began with a book entitled *Shakespeare Restored*, implying that Shakespeare's *Folio* had suffered in the faulty copying of the several seventeenth-century editions and the arbitrary handiwork of Pope. Theobald wrote in his introduction to *Shakespeare Restored* that through "*Indolence*" and "*Ignorance* of his EDITORS, we have scarce any Book in the *English* Tongue more fertile of Errors" and that he felt a need to "[retrieve], as far as possible, the original *Purity* of his *Text*, and root out that vast Crop of *Errors*, which has almost choak'd up his *Beauties*" (Br).[20] Efforts to recover Shakespeare's text had begun. A growing number of people interested in the study of Shakespeare meant that publications upon his text would require a method of inquiry that satisfied an audience of intellectual and interested readers. Thus, Theobald justified the emendations that he made in his text with explanations, and even if all were not correct, they were sincere attempts at presenting Shakespeare's text as worthy of study.[21] Its worthiness for Theobald, suggests Peter Seary, is in the language and character that Shakespeare masters, moving readers away from "neo-Aristotelian preoccupations with plot or fable" (32).

Textual editing of *Coriolanus* has been concerned primarily with mislinings, spelling, and other surface errors, and even the mislinings may hardly make a difference in a reading of the text. Lines ending on unexpected words might have been the result of the compositors' having to end lines where no space was left, and in that event, a new line might have been started. The compositors might have copied Shakespeare's foul papers as Shakespeare had written them, and if they did, why Shakespeare would have broken a pentameter line is not clear. Philip Brockbank sums up well what an editor of *Coriolanus* will find true of the *Folio* text:

1. that while over three hundred lines are irregularly divided, over two thousand are within the pentameter norm;
2. that while transitions are often a problem, the greater number are regular;
3. that the higher incidence of apparent mislinings is in A's stint;

4. that A, more markedly than B, tends to set irregular verse in syntactical rather than metrical units.[22]

Knowing how the text was set and by whom allows readers to see that the transmission of *Coriolanus* from Shakespeare's foul papers to the *Folio* was complicated by compositor practices in setting and printing. If Shakespeare were alive when the *Folio* was published, perhaps he might have been able to let all know what the final product should present to us. In the meantime, the authority of students of Shakespeare's *Folio* will suffice.

No stage history of the play exists prior to the Restoration. Dating of the play is conjectured upon some historical data: crop dearths in England in 1607 and 1608, the freezing of the Thames in 1607–1608, and an allusion from Ben Jonson's *Epicoene*.[23] Whether or not it was coincidence that Shakespeare wrote a play that alludes to contemporary events, we cannot be sure; however, lacking a date of performance or registration, entertaining contemporary allusions, as well as situating the play in relation to other works in Shakespeare's repertoire, is a plausible way to narrow a date. The corn dearth that is mentioned in *Coriolanus*, although it is also mentioned in Shakespeare's primary source, Plutarch's *Lives*, may well echo contemporary events. A grain shortage appeared to lead to rebelliousness among England's citizenry. An entry in the *Proclamation Book* for June 2, 1607, notes that there is a "Dearth of corn in Warwickshire" and that "The common people threaten to resist turning arable land into pasture."[24] The Midland Revolt in May 1607 included Northamptonshire and Leicestershire, not only Warwickshire, home to Shakespeare's family at Stratford-on-Avon. In these communities, farmers faced losing open farm land to "enclosed" pasture for sheep. John Dover Wilson finds that based upon these events early 1608 is a likely date for *Coriolanus*.[25] Other indicators that the play might have been written in 1608 include events not only in the rural areas, however, but also in London. Leah S. Marcus writes that barges of grain were unloaded at the Tower of London, where customs were collected and from where grain was dispersed. During the famine of 1607 and 1608, questions over who received the customs, court officials or the city of London, led to arguments between the two separate governing bodies, the city feeling that the court was unfairly profiting from customs. Moreover, shippers were being overcharged by Tower officials who exacted "personal percentages," and thus costs eventually trickled down to the citizens.[26] Marcus sees these events being played out in *Coriolanus*, with Martius's patrician disregard for the plebeians' hunger and their inability to afford high grain prices.

The freezing over of the Thames in 1607–1608, a highly unusual event, is captured in *The Great Frost* (1608), presumably by Thomas Dekker. In it is mention of "pans of coals" sitting halfway across the frozen ice to "warm your fingers," to which line 1.1.172 in *Coriolanus* is thought to allude: "the coal of fire upon the ice."[27] In Dekker's work, the pans of ice are mentioned as means to showing how much the Thames has turned "the goodliest river in the whole kingdom into the broadest street to walk in."[28] The river is as busy as a London street, with sellers and buyers of goods.

Such a phenomenon, to be sure, would live long in the memories of those who crossed it or saw it. Dekker mentions that the freeze lasted from December 1607 through January 1608. What it engendered in Shakespeare's imagination can only be surmised. Looking at the context in which this line appears, we see that Shakespeare put to very different use the idea of coals on ice. Caius Martius Coriolanus, telling a group of rebellious citizens how inconstant they were, claimed that they "were no surer, no, / than is the coal of fire upon the ice, / or hailstone in the sun" (1.1.171–73). Fire/sun and ice/hailstone are juxtaposed. The sun will melt hail as quickly as the ice will put out the coal. That is how changeable Martius found the common citizens of Rome. In Dekker's text, the idea that coals of fire were kept upon a river excites wonder, and seems little related to Martius's pithy insult. But then again, in Dekker's text, themes of hunger and cold among the poor drive the conversation between a Citizen of London and "an old Countryman" about the Great Frost. The citizen tells the countryman how hard and persistent has been the ice on the Thames since before Christmas, that even a short thaw was not able to "dissolve so great a hardness," that once the "cakes of ice, great in quantity and in great numbers, were made and baked cold in the mouth of winter . . . they were crusted and cemented together; but after they had joined their strengths into one, their backs held out and could not be broken."[29] The countryman responds that an analogy suggests itself: "London upholdeth a State: and again, that violent factions and combinations, albeit of the basest persons, in a commonwealth are not easily dissolved; if once they be suffered to grow upon a head."[30]

In this comment, a central theme in *Coriolanus* is evident: political control as perceived by the wealthy and the poor. The patricians, or wealthy citizens, retain control of Rome, but during Martius's time, the plebeians, or people, have some representation in government. Martius takes issue with the citizens' having a voice or vote at all. He feels that the senate takes care of its citizens, including the plebeians, and that the plebeians should be grateful; left to rule themselves, claims Martius, the plebeians "would feed on one another" (1.1.187). As for the countryman's analogy concerning the dissolution of strong factions, in Martius's Rome, the plebeians have not yet reached that level of political maturity. After Martius rants at the rebellious plebeians and sends them home, he tells his friend Menenius that another group of rebellious plebeians in the city "are dissolv'd" (1.1.203). That "violent faction" apparently had backs that did not hold out, and that could still be broken.

Certainly news and comments upon social unrest and social justice in circulation in London and other English communities during the late sixteenth and early seventeenth centuries might easily be transmitted into the mouths of dramatic characters, and in turn might help situate a play's date. In a country whose people were divided on the issue of social rights and government control, images invoked by analogies such as the old countryman's were imaginative visuals that supported a speaker's ideas. One of the more prevalent analogies during the period was that of the human body and the monarchy. The king was the head, his people or state the body. The king ruled the people the way that a head ruled the body, and during James I's reign, the king believed that he ruled by divine right. Thus, when the old countryman suggests that the commonwealth will not be easily dissolved once they are allowed to grow upon a head, he is mimicking the popular view of the head of state as being in political control.

James I came to the throne in 1603, and because some ideas present in *Coriolanus* were in circulation at the time, we can date the play after 1603. One reason for a date of no later than 1608 is an allusion to the play from a play that was staged in 1609–1610, Ben Jonson's *Epicœne or The Silent Woman*. Jonson's Truewit says at line 5.4.227, "you have lurched your friends of the better part of the garland, by concealing this part of the plot." Bullough claims this is a "jesting allusion" to a line in *Coriolanus* which says that Martius "lurched all swords of the garland" (2.2.101).[31] Another play that cannot be dated, as it likewise was not known to be staged during Shakespeare's lifetime, is *Antony and Cleopatra*. Critics have had to count on allusions in other dated plays to arrive at the 1607 or 1608 date often affixed to that tragedy. Whether one was written before, after, or in conjunction with the other, the fact is, without a staging date, it makes little difference in what order they are placed. That they both use Plutarch's *Lives* as a primary source, both have passionate Roman warriors as their subjects, and both are complex, political plays of Shakespeare's maturity hints at their being written one after the other; thus, the 1607–1608 periods may be regarded as fairly accurate dates.

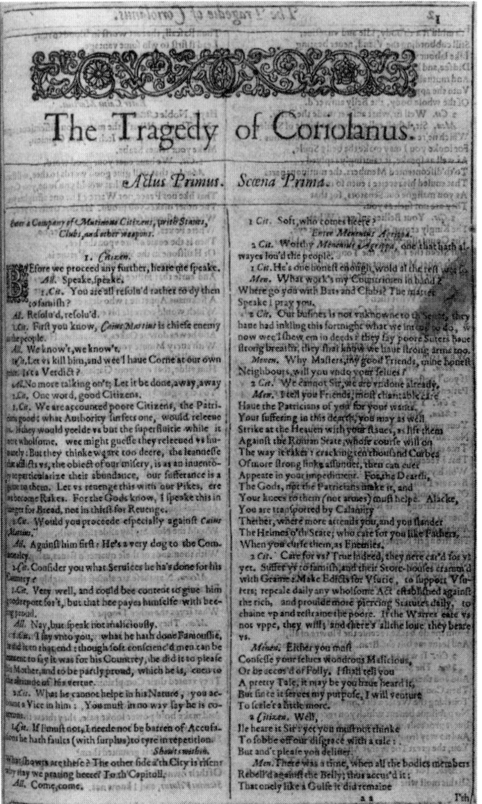

The Tragedy of Coriolanus.

Actus Primus. Scœna Prima.

Enter a Company of Mutinous Citizens, with Staues, Clubs, and other weapons.

1. *Citizen.*

BEfore we proceed any further, heare me speake.

All. Speake, speake.

1.Cit. You are all resolu'd rather to dy then to famish?

All. Resolu'd, resolu'd.

1.Cit. First you know, *Caius Martius* is chiefe enemy to the people.

All. We know't, we know't.

1.Cit. Let vs kill him, and wee'l haue Corne at our own price. Is't a Verdict?

All. No more talking on't; Let it be done, away, away

2.Cit. One word, good Citizens.

1.Cit. We are accounted poore Citizens, the Patricians good: what Authority surfets one, would releeue vs. If they would yeelde vs but the superfluitie while it were wholsome, wee might guesse they releeued vs humanely: But they thinke we are too deere, the leannesse that afflicts vs, the obiect of our misery, is as an inuentory to particularize their abundance, our sufferance is a gaine to them. Let vs reuenge this with our Pikes, ere we become Rakes. For the Gods know, I speake this in hunger for Bread, not in thirst for Reuenge.

2.Cit. Would you proceede especially against *Caius Martius.*

All. Against him first: He's a very dog to the Commonalty.

2.Cit. Consider you what Seruices he ha's done for his Countrey?

1.Cit. Very well, and could bee content to giue him good report for't, but that hee payes himselfe with beeing proud.

All. Nay, but speak not maliciously.

1.Cit. I say vnto you, what he hath done Famouslie, he did it to that end: though soft conscienc'd men can be content to say it was for his Countrey, he did it to please his Mother, and to be partly proud, which he is, euen to the altitude of his vertue.

2.Cit. What he cannot helpe in his Nature, you account a Vice in him: You must in no way say he is couetous.

1.Cit. If I must not, I neede not be barren of Accusations he hath faults (with surplus) to tyre in repetition.

Showts within.

What showts are these? The other side a'th City is risen: why stay we prating heere? To th'Capitoll.

All. Come, come.

1 Cit. Soft, who comes heere?

Enter Menenius Agrippa.

2 Cit. Worthy *Menenius Agrippa*, one that hath alwayes lou'd the people.

1 Cit. He's one honest enough, wold al the rest were so.

Men. What work's my Countrimen in hand? Where go you with Bats and Clubs? The matter Speake I pray you.

2 Cit. Our busines is not vnknowne to th'Senat, they haue had inkling this fortnight what we intend to do, we now wee'l shew em in deeds: they say poore Suters haue strong breaths, they shal know we haue strong arms too.

Menen. Why Masters, my good Friends, mine honest Neighbours, will you vndo your selues?

2 Cit. We cannot Sir, we are vndone already.

Men. I tell you Friends, most charitable care Haue the Patricians of you for your wants. Your suffering in this dearth, you may as well Strike at the Heauen with your staues, as lift them Against the Roman State, whose course will on The way it takes: cracking ten thousand Curbes Of more strong linke assunder, then can euer Appeare in your impediment. For the Dearth, The Gods, not the Patricians make it, and Your knees to them (not armes) must helpe. Alacke, You are transported by Calamity Thether, where more attends you, and you slander The Helmes o'th State; who care for you like Fathers, When you curse them, as Enemies.

2 Cit. Care for vs? True indeed, they nere car'd for vs yet. Suffer vs to famish, and their Store-houses cramm'd with Graine: Make Edicts for Vsurie, to support Vsurers; repeale daily any wholsome Act established against the rich, and prouide more piercing Statutes daily, to chaine vp and restraine the poore. If the Warres eate vs not vppe, they will; and there's all the loue they beare vs.

Menen. Either you must Confesse your selues wondrous Malicious, Or be accus'd of Folly. I shall tell you A pretty Tale, it may be you haue heard it, But since it serues my purpose, I will venture To scale't a little more.

2 Citizen. Well, Ile heare it Sir: yet you must not thinke To fobbe off our disgrace with a tale: But and't please you deliuer.

Men. There was a time, when all the bodies members Rebell'd against the Belly; thus accus'd it: That onely like a Gulfe it did remaine

aa Th'

STC 22273 copy 52. First Folio, 1623. First page of *Coriolanus*. By Permission of the Folger Shakespeare Library.

NOTES

1. Geoffrey Bullough, ed., *Narrative and Dramatic Sources of Shakespeare, V: The Roman Plays*, 8 vols. (London: Routledge, 1964), p. 453.

2. From Helge Kökeritz, ed., *Mr. William Shakespeare's Comedies, Histories, & Tragedies: A Facsimile Edition* (New Haven, CT: Yale UP, [1623] 1954), also known as the *First Folio*, sig. A3. Any reference to the facsimile will be cited as Kökeritz. I have regularized the spelling.

3. The names of two of the companies for which Shakespeare played and wrote, writes W. W. Greg, *The Shakespeare First Folio: Its Bibliographical and Textual History* (Oxford: Clarendon Press, 1955), pp. 81–89.

4. Greg, *Shakespeare First Folio*, p. 159.

5. E. K. Chambers, *William Shakespeare: The Elizabethan Stage*, 4 vols. (Oxford: Clarendon, 1930), 3:193; Greg, *Shakespeare First Folio*, p. 159.

6. Fredson Bowers, *On Editing Shakespeare and Elizabethan Dramatists* (Philadelphia: Pennsylvania, 1955), p. 13, uses the term *foul papers* for the final draft rather than the term *fair copy*.

7. Bowers, *On Editing*, suggests that copies of manuscripts could be sent to the compositor for printing in a number of ways: as an author's fair copy or finished draft, a scribe's version of the author's foul papers, scribal copies from the promptbook, the manuscript promptbook, and an earlier printed edition, for instance, p. 12.

8. Greg, *Shakespeare First Folio*, p. 427, says the copy is from foul papers. Bowers, *On Editing*, believes that dramatists probably sent fair copy, finished and ready for transcription for the promptbook, rather than foul papers (18). Given the evidence to date, it is reasonable to assume that a manuscript or foul copy was used by the compositors.

9. Charleton Hinman, *The Printing and Proofreading of the First Folio of Shakespeare*, 2 vols. (Oxford: Clarendon, 1963), tells us that Compositor A and Compositor B can be distinguished by A's habit of spelling "doe," "goe," and "here," and B's habit of spelling each "do," "go," and "heere," pp. 182–84.

10. See J. Dover Wilson's "The New Way with Shakespeare's Texts: An Introduction for Lay Readers," *Shakespeare Survey* 9 (1956): 69–80, for an illuminating essay on problems associated with editing Shakespeare's works in general.

11. See note 9.

12. According to Ronald B. McKerrow, *The Treatment of Shakespeare's Text by His Earlier Editors: 1709–1768* (Folcraft, PA: Folcraft Press, 1939), p. 4, the *Second Folio* was published in 1632 and the *Third Folio* was published in 1663.

13. Thomas R. Lounsbury, *The First Editors of Shakespeare: Pope and Theobald* (Folcraft, PA: Folcraft Library Editions, [1906] 1974), p. 71. McKerrow, *Treatment of Shakespeare's Text*, p. 5, cites updating of spellings and typographical errors as being typical in the various folios.

14. Samuel Holt Monk, intro., "Some Account of the Life of Mr. William Shakespeare (1709) by Nicholas Rowe," *The Augustan Reprint Society Publications* 17 (1948) (rpt. by Kraus Reprint Society, 1967), p. 1.

15. Ibid., p. 1.

16. Pope used Rowe's edition as the basis of his edition, according to McKerrow, *Treatment of Shakespeare's Text*, p. 17.

17. Harry Levin, "Critical Approaches to Shakespeare from 1660 to 1904," in *The Cambridge Companion to Shakespeare Studies*, ed. Stanley Wells (Cambridge, England: Cambridge UP, 1986), p. 217, says that "techniques of scholarship" marked the work by later editors Lewis Theobold (1733), Edward Capell (1768), and Edmond Malone (1790).

18. Lounsbury, *First Editors of Shakespeare*, p. 106.

19. See Chapter 2, "Contexts and Sources."

20. Theobald's first book concerned itself mostly with *Hamlet*. According to McKerrow, *Treatment of Shakespeare's Text*, pp. 23–24, his finished edition of Shakespeare's works appeared in 1733.

21. Levin, *Critical Approaches*, p. 217; Lounsbury, *First Editors of Shakespeare*, p. 179.

22. Philip Brockbank is the editor of the edition of *Coriolanus* I cite in this study, *Coriolanus: The Arden Shakespeare* (London: Methuen, 1976). The introduction to the textual problems of the play is lucidly presented in the *Arden*, and it is a good place to begin further investigation of Shakespeare's *Coriolanus*.

23. Bullough, *Narrative and Dramatic Sources*, pp. 453–54. The threat of loss of land combined with fears of hunger drove the revolts, as Lee Bliss, ed., *Coriolanus* (Cambridge, England: Cambridge UP, 2000), p. 17, concludes.

24. Great Britain, Public Record Office, *Calendar of State Papers, Domestic Series, of the Reigns of Edward VI, Mary, Elizabeth [and James I] 1547–1625*, 12 vols., ed. Robert Lemon (Nedeln, Liechtenstein: Kraus Reprint, 1967), 8:437.

25. From John Dover Wilson, ed., *The Tragedy of Coriolanus* (Cambridge, England: Cambridge UP, 1960).

26. Leah S. Marcus, "*Coriolanus* and the Expansion of City Liberties," in *Shakespeare's Late Tragedies: A Collection of Critical Essays*, ed. Susan L. Wofford (New York: Prentice-Hall, 1996), p. 190.

27. Bullough, *Narrative and Dramatic Sources*, p. 562

28. Ibid., p. 562.

29. Ibid., p. 561.

30. Ibid., p. 561.

31. Ibid., p. 454. M. W. MacCallum, in *Shakespeare's Roman Plays and Their Background* (London: Macmillan, 1910; rpt. London: Macmillan, 1935), notes that the term *lurched* was in use at the time, so Jonson's using it is not unusual. The term used with the phrase *of the garland* is what suggests that Jonson was "girding" one of Shakespeare's plays, as MacCallum, p. 460, says is probable.

2

CONTEXTS AND SOURCES

CONTEXTS

The playhouse and amphitheater tradition in late sixteenth-century London was only three decades old when Shakespeare wrote *Coriolanus*, and in that time, dramatic forms and genres developed that shaped the early modern English stage and distinguished it from all earlier performance arts and later theatrical periods. The lack of women players, for instance, or the fact that plays were written with theatrical companies and its individual players in mind—or even monarchical censorship—suggests the limitations that might have imposed themselves upon the dramatist. But these limitations were in fact traditions known and understood well by the time Shakespeare wrote *Coriolanus*. *Coriolanus* is indebted to an evolving theatrical tradition; at the same time, the tragedy is also the product of a growing interest in the translation into English of ancient Roman literature and historical narratives. Not to be ignored is the genre of tragedy as it evolved within the theatrical tradition in early modern England.

Prior to 1576, when hall playhouses were first constructed in England in the London suburbs,[1] secular theatrical entertainment in London was performed by groups of players or entertainers in public spaces, such as inn yards,[2] or in private houses. Before the reign of Henry VIII, playing or acting in England was usually religious—moralities and saints' plays, for instance, were acted annually by guild members during the cycle of Roman Catholic holy days or feasts and guided by church authorities or clerics. Henry VIII's break with the Catholic Church changed the tenor of those plays, however, as references to the pope, in some instances, had to be purged. Glynne Wickham et al. point us to this form of censorship as more or less the beginning of the English government's interest in playmaking, religious or secular, as being potentially threatening to the established social order of rank.[3]

Throughout the reign of Edward VI (1547–1553) and Mary (1553–1558), proclamations either banning interludes and entertainments or censoring them were issued, revoked, and amended, as fears persisted over sedition, no doubt fueled by the religious controversies of the period.[4]

During Elizabeth I's (1558–1603) reign, however, the theater flourished. Like her successor, Elizabeth I was a supporter of the theater; at the same time, she established controls over players and playing. Laws against "vagabondage" enacted in Henry's reign were reenacted during Elizabeth's. Such laws made it illegal for players to perform unless they belonged to the household of a nobleman or had permission from local justices.[5] Because the vagabond laws named those whose livelihood was not attached to a guild or other lawfully acknowledged business, such as peddlers, we see at this time that players had yet to be taken seriously, that dramatic performance had yet to be considered a profession. That soon changed, as players and plays proved popular. Theater companies, as the groups of actors who played on the early modern stage came to be called, sprang up in rural and urban areas alike. In London, plays were popular with citizens, too, which led to a number of problems that made necessary the building of permanent structures for the companies. Traffic congestion and crime within the city increased near the inns during performances, making the companies unpopular with London city leaders. London leaders were also annoyed that the plays attracted the sizeable audiences of young tradesmen and others who authorities felt should be spending their money in established London shops, working, or going to Church. Early in Elizabeth's reign, on December 6, 1574, a statute concerning plays and other entertainments was enacted, its contents summing up the chief concerns of authorities and others in communities where theatrical performances were most likely to affect church-going (required of citizens), working, spending money, moral behavior, or public safety:

> Whereas heretofore sundry great disorders and inconveniences have been found to ensue to this City by the inordinate haunting of great multitudes of people, specially youth, to plays, enterludes, and shows, namely occasion of frays and quarrels, evil practices of incontinency in great inns, having chambers and secret places adjoining to their open stages and galleries, inveighing and alluring of

> maids, specially orphans and good citizens' children under age, to privy and unmeet contracts, the publishing of unchaste, uncomely and unshamefast speeches and doings, withdrawing of the Queen's Majesty's subjects from divine service on Sundays and Holydays—at which times such plays were chiefly used—unthrifty waste of the money of the poor and fond persons; sundry robberies by picking and cutting of purses; uttering of popular, busy and seditious matters; and many other corruptions of youth, and other enormities besides that also sundry slaughters and mayhemmings of the Queen's subjects have happened by ruins of scaffolds, frames and stages, and by engines, weapons and powder used in plays. (Wickam 73–74)

The notion that theatrical entertainments triggered a host of social ills and social behaviors thought unwholesome indicates that the establishment's perception of playing was that it was not much better an occupation or avocation than many nonlegitimate practices. Indeed, one of the reasons women were not allowed to play was to prevent them from being exploited, not to mention that the acting trade was elitist—controlling the organization and structure of a company kept membership low and subsequently kept money channeled to fewer individuals, as we shall soon see. Moreover, the recognition in the same act that good plays acted for the queen or for public good were considered acceptable leads us to conclude that if plays did not draw large crowds or cost money to watch or stir sedition, then they would have gone unnoticed by the governing officials.

Elizabeth I's court, however, showed support for the theater groups, licensing them, and in effect regulating their activities.[6] Once they were licensed, companies' plays were subject to scrutiny and censorship by the Master of the Revels, who from 1581 onward was given the office of overseeing all plays and performers in England. In this context, plays written for the stage were dominated by consideration for who would play parts, what could be written, or where and when plays could be performed.

Statutes governing the control and structure of theaters and theater companies succeeded in limiting the number of companies and theater buildings and closing the doors to theaters during plagues, Sundays, Lent, and holy days—most of the time. The acts were violated often enough to cause lawsuits periodically. As theater companies found permanent places to play, and they themselves became highly structured, they developed for themselves a reputation of respect and legitimacy by the time *Coriolanus* would have been staged. Antitheatricalists waged war against the stage until all theaters were closed, but they seemed not to have much effect on the dramatist of the leading company in London, the King's Men.

Theater companies saw a need to control the structure of a company from the number of members to the wage scale. Apprenticing boys at around the age of ten,[7] the men's companies were composed of masters or members, the apprentices, and hired men, a total of around thirty-five.[8] The masters were permanent members, the apprentices were those who worked toward becoming masters,[9] and the hired men were those who were not likely to become members, as the openings for masters were rare and being an apprentice was no guarantee of becoming a member in any company. Shakespeare's company, which would have been the Kings' Men from 1603 to 1641, is known to have had only twelve members at any given time, Shakespeare being one (47–48), although he is not known to have played principal roles.[10] Prior to being the Kings' Men, Shakespeare's company was known as the Lord Chamberlain's Men, when Elizabeth I had responsibility of them,[11] and the members numbered only nine. As a rule, the members played the men's roles, the apprentices played the women's roles, and the hired men played the less important male roles.[12] The structure of the organization remained such until the closing of the theaters in 1642; only when a member died could an apprentice rise to the position of member. Thus, the group of actors who were to perform *Coriolanus* probably had long worked together on Shakespeare's plays. Although there are no complete lists of who played what parts in Shakespeare's plays, other material evidence suggests that Richard Burbage played Caius Martius Coriolanus. Burbage was a young man in 1590 who came to be a principal actor among the members, usually playing the tragic hero in Shakespeare's tragedies.

T. W. Baldwin argues that dramatists wrote plays with the companies and actors in mind. As the number of licensed companies in London was only about five during the period Shakespeare wrote, there was a set number of actors, of talent, with which a dramatist could work.[13] As Baldwin writes, "[t]he company was not fitted to the play, but the play to the company" (300). Shakespeare knew that when he wrote a tragic hero, Richard Burbage was likely to play the part. Thus, the hero who played Hamlet, Lear, or Antony was also going to play Martius.[14] Burbage, about eighteen years an actor when Shakespeare wrote the play, probably could have played Martius any number of ways, so we know that Shakespeare probably felt no limitation in creating Martius's character. The role of Volumnia would have required a skilled actor, and it appears that Shakespeare had one—we know he needed one for Cleopatra in the year prior. Around the probable time the play was written, changes in the company organization and in the place where a play took place occurred. Blackfriar's, a hall-style theater that had long housed a children's acting company, was purchased by Shakespeare's company in 1608. Shakespeare's company hired two of the children's company's actors, according to Baldwin, actors favored by the patrons of the theater, perhaps as a means to securing the clientele.[15] This move appears to have been profitable to Shakespeare and his fellow shareholders.[16] How this might have affected Shakespeare's writing of *Coriolanus* can only be conjectured, but we are reminded that Shakespeare had expectations of success and profit.

SOURCES

Crafting characters for the early modern stage using personages from historical narrative was by no means new to Shakespeare. He had culled British chronicles for the stories of Lancastrian and Yorkist monarchs and nobles for his history plays. From the Greek Plutarch, whose *Lives of Famous Grecians and Romanes* was translated into English in 1579 by Thomas North, Shakespeare found a wealth of material for *Julius Caesar* (1599) and his last three tragedies: *Antony and Cleopatra* (1607–1608), *Timon* (1607–1608), and *Coriolanus* (1608–1609). Another account of Martius's life available to Shakespeare was Philemon Holland's 1600 translation into English of *The Romane History of T. Livy*,[17] but Plutarch seems to be the primary source, given Shakespeare's liberal use of his biographies for tragedies written during the same time period.

Coriolanus is the last tragedy that Shakespeare wrote, and certainly the last to have as its subject a tragic Roman hero. Thus, in the development of Martius, we see the experienced hand of a dramatist who had been creating Roman and other tragic heroes for the stage since the early 1590s, not to mention one who had the opportunity to see how his contemporaries were translating figures from the Roman past into dramatic characters for London audiences, coterie and popular alike. Roman plays, while not necessarily a definitive genre, were written by a considerable number of dramatists of the period 1585–1635. Forty-three known plays by authors of tragedies and histories, not to mention of romances, included Roman characters and settings,[18] although it was when Shakespeare's own *Julius Caesar* was staged that Roman plays on stage were becoming popular.[19]

The motivations for writing about Roman figures, as well as the source material, differed among the early modern dramatists. In the instance of *Sejanus, His Fall*, possibly one of the best Roman-themed tragedies of the period, Ben Jonson was most interested in writing a historically accurate tragedy, so much so that he cited his sources in the margins of his tragedy. On the other hand, Shakespeare seems not to have concerned himself with historical accuracy as much as he concerned himself with developing tragic character that would be attractive to London audiences. Shakespeare's *Coriolanus* is a consciously English reconstruction of a Roman historical figure and setting, as we find in the play those anachronisms that remind us that Shakespeare was writing about historical figures that would be recognized by audiences as characters from the past being played by actors that they had seen play numerous other roles. Thus, calling two plebeians "Hob and Dick" or having the plebeians and patricians throwing their caps in the air (what kind of caps were worn by ancient Romans in Shakespeare's mind?) or "matrons" "[flinging] gloves" (did Roman matrons wear gloves?) or even having the plebeians speaking in Jacobean English signaled to audiences that they were being referred to a historical past while they watched in the historical present. Whereas Jonson was interested in reconstituting history in a tragedy as a means to validate English drama through accurate, historical facts,[20] Shakespeare was content to exploit history for aesthetic purposes and paying audiences.

Why Roman-themed plays were popular with dramatists or other artists is open to conjecture, but it appears English writers and thinkers had already begun to show interest in ancient Roman culture and the lessons that might be learned from the past as early as the medieval period. In English medieval plays could be found Tiberius, Augustus, and Pilate (Ronan 17), figures from scripture and secular works. The Roman Empire extended at one time into England, leaving evidence of their intrusion into the far western isle in their roadways, forts, coins, and tombstones.[21] The myth of Brutus, legendary founder of Britain and the grandson of Aeneas, the legendary founder of Rome, was repeated in the sixteenth- and seventeenth-century chronicles on English history by Raphael Holinshed or Richard Grafton or Camden that were popularized by Geoffrey of Monmouth in *History of the Kings of Britain* (1136). Rome represented to Britains power and savagery. Early moderns knew that the androcentric Romans were aggressive, brutal, violent, martial, and self-serving from Lucan and Tacitus, from Ovid and Livy.[22] They also knew the "classic" model of the duty-minded, loyal, devoted man of the Roman state that we see in Virgil's Aeneas. *Pietas* is the term used to describe loyalty to family, the state, and the gods.[23] The Roman *virtus*, or manliness, was supported by the Roman virtues of *dignitas, constantia,* and *integritas*.[24] And in a country with a growing interest in nation-building and imperialism, as was Shakespeare's, the Romans of Julius and Augustus Caesar's Rome were attractive, as Ronan points out, for "England found in Rome a glass where the island could behold its own image simultaneously civilized and barbarous" (7). Moreover, the "discord" that is seen between the patricians and plebeians of Rome, thinks Charles Wells, "mirrored the social and political unease that ran like a dark thread through so much of Elizabeth's reign" (5).

MacCullum suggests that next to English history, which Shakespeare famously re-created in his history plays during Elizabeth's reign, classical history was popular with early modern English people, and Roman history more than Greek, which may explain in part Shakespeare's turning toward Roman themes for his tragedies (76). England's interest in defining itself as a nation, its throwing off the yoke of the papacy, and its desire for social order and stability, suggests MacCullum, are also plausible reasons for sixteenth-century Englishmen looking to a past culture that valued ideals of state unity and social order (76). The Roman figures' role as subjects of misfortune, however, possibly was key to Shakespeare's interest in them as tragic subjects. The early moderns understood tragedy as demonstrating a "change from happiness to misery."[25] Roman historical narratives, among others, provided exemplars or models of fortune and misfortune. The virtuous and less-than-virtuous political behavior of the ancient Romans had become attractive to writers during the Italian Renaissance, whose works in turn influenced other European writers.[26] Boccaccio's *De casibus virorum illustrium* (1355–1374), translated by England's John Lydgate and entitled *The Fall of Princes* (1438),[27] "was one of the most influential versions of history the Renaissance produced."[28] Wolfgang Iser said that Boccaccio's *De casibus* was enormously popular because people who were used to theological explanations for human existence were increasingly interested in the "inescapability" of fortune or chance in human affairs: all ranks of society in Boccaccio's effort were subject to chance, rising only to fall. Lydgate, suggested Iser, saw the possibility of people having some control over fortune, by not allowing fortune to "impose its effects" on individual lives.[29]

The *de casibus* tradition brought to England by Lydgate found an audience in and influenced the literary work of a group of men who wrote a series of verse narratives in a collection entitled the *Mirror for Magistrates*. Edited by William Baldwin and published in 1559, the *Mirror*'s purpose was stated at the outset: to show princes how to govern. Thus, the lives of famous and notorious political English men and women, such as Richard III, Owen Glendower, Hastings, and Jane Shore, were related in first-person narratives. Each figure recounted his or her tale of misfortune, most recognizing the combination of fate and individual choices that led to their undoing or their tragedies. Undoubtedly, Shakespeare knew the *Mirror*, whose many characters appear in his histories. In the 1587 edition of the *Mirror*, edited by John Higgins, Roman figures too appeared, such as Julius Caesar, Tiberius, Caligula, and Claudius. Stories about Roman rulers were popular with writers who saw England's pedigree in the Romans.

The *de casibus* figure was well known by the time that the theater was developing. Also known to Shakespeare were the mystery cycles, dramatizations of biblical narratives that were popularized in the fourteenth and fifteenth centuries and still played in the sixteenth.[30] Emrys Jones suggests one cycle play, *The Passion*, which tells the story of Christ's life from the Last Supper to his death, "stands out for its tragic or quasi-tragic impact" (47). Brutus and Sicinius's sentencing of Martius in Act Three of *Coriolanus* contains parallels to Pontius Pilate, thinks Jones (62), as one instance when Shakespeare might have recalled staging of the mystery cycle from his youth.

At the same time, ideas about representation of characters and ideas in literature and drama were in circulation. In *A Defence of Poetry* (1586), Philip Sidney referenced Greek classical drama as a model, claiming that Aristotle's "precept" was that "the stage should always represent but one place and . . . one day" (65), a pattern Sidney felt was violated too often by early modern dramatists. Representing history, Sidney thought, could be accomplished with the use of a *nuntius* to announce or report time and place, and dramatists should not begin a dramatic interpretation *ab ovo*, but on an event that was the subject of the drama (66). What was known about Aristotle and *Poetics* in the early modern period is not entirely clear; for instance, of the "unities" of time, place, and action, characteristics of tragedy adhered to by neoclassicists of the Renaissance and Restoration,[31] the *Poetics* only mentions unity of action.

Aristotle's *Poetics* is a collection of notes that Aristotle may or may not have intended to publish. What scholars study today may or may not have been edited by others, and because the collected notes are often difficult to understand out of context, what scholars study depends on the translation or translations under consideration. The three books that Aristotle wrote, *On Poets*, have never been found; they are known to exist through other writers who had access to them.[32]

In the *Poetics*, Aristotle wrote that "tragedy is an imitation of an action that is admirable, complete and possesses magnitude; in language made pleasurable, each of its species separated in different parts; performed by actors, not through narration; effecting through pity and fear the purification of such emotions" (Aristotle 10). Plot was most important to Aristotle in that it "imitated" the actions of a character or characters, preferably invented characters and events rather than historical figures and events (Aristotle 16). Aristotle thought "that the function of the poet [was] not to say what *has* happened, but to say the kind of thing that *would* happen" (Aristotle 16). For Aristotle, plots could be simple or complex. In a simple plot, a change from, say, good fortune to bad fortune might occur, but no reversal or recognition on the part of a character was necessary. In a complex plot, a reversal, recognition, or both were desired. A reversal was a change in the actions that were being shown. Reversal occurring with recognition, the change from a state of ignorance to a state of knowledge, Aristotle thought, was ideal, especially as both would excite pity and fear (Aristotle 18–19). A chorus and song usually attended the tragedy Aristotle defined (Aristotle 19–20). One of the most well-known and controversial ideas advanced by Aristotle was that of *hamartia*, or error. Some have interpreted the error to mean a moral flaw possessed by the protagonist, a flaw that leads to his or her tragic ending; in the *Poetics*, Aristotle says that a "change to bad fortune . . . is not due to any moral defect or depravity, but to an error of some kind" (Aristotle 21).

Plot as imitation of action, reversal, recognition, the exciting of pity and fear, the idea of an error, a chorus—these were just a few of the important components of tragedy that Aristotle articulated, and though we can find in *Coriolanus* an imitation of an action that evokes pity and fear, the play is based upon a historical figure whose life is reconstructed in a dramatic format for viewer consumption. Caius Martius's fortunes turn on him because of his inability to compromise his personal values to satisfy his fellow Romans, not because he is morally depraved (at least according to Roman morals). We can say that his error is in his seeking revenge on Rome, but never do we see Martius recognizing this as something that he should not have considered. Perhaps that is because he never fully commits the error. If there is no error and no recognition of one, then is the play flawed? One problem in looking at *Coriolanus* from an Aristotelian or neo-Aristotelian orientation is that it can lead to critics and others seeing weaknesses rather than strengths in the play, as did Restoration dramatists who altered the play to adhere to neoclassical ideas about dramatic structure (see Chapter 6).[33]

What is true about reading ancient texts or early modern drama is that it is an act of interpretation, and different generations of writers and critics have interpreted Shakespeare and Aristotle to suit a number of political or social interests or interrogations into aesthetic forms. When Shakespeare wrote *Coriolanus*, he was, in essence, interpreting a number of aesthetic forms and ideas about those forms passed on to him, as well as developing popular themes and styles in theatrical performance. Those threads of the past woven into his work are intriguing to investigate, because they show how rich a pattern emerged in the final product. As we have no evidence from Shakespeare that articulates his ideas about Aristotle, *de casibus* figures, morality plays, the ancient Greeks or the Romans as influences, being aware of what Shakespeare might have known or appreciated creates for us a context within which to interpret his texts, just as do the primary and other sources for his plays. Coming from histories, figures like Julius Caesar, Antony, and Caius Martius are transformed into tragic characters in these Roman plays.

Although other sources of Roman antiquity were available to dramatists, North's Plutarch was popular, already in its third edition by the time Shakespeare wrote *Coriolanus.* Plutarch's importance in the development of Shakespeare's *Coriolanus* cannot be understated. The Greek ancient Plutarch not only provided the biographical material that informs the characters in *Coriolanus* but also, as a widely admired author of stories of Roman and Greek antiquity, provided early modern dramatists with a number of exemplary historical figures whose lives, not to mention their governments, might be mirrors of their own time. Plutarch was one of many "authorities" on ancient Roman life and culture enjoyed by sixteenth-century English writers and readers. Another, Livy, is a possible source, and not merely because of Holland's translation into English. Shakespeare's early education introduced him to *Ab Urbe Condita*, in which Livy told of republican Rome and Caius Martius Coriolanus. The fable of the belly used in Shakespeare could be Livy's version,[34] though it might not be Shakespeare's single source for the fable.[35] Livy was not new to Shakespeare when he wrote *Coriolanus* in the early seventeenth century.[36] Livy on republican Rome was the authority the English recognized; indeed, Livy was the historian that Plutarch was not.[37]

Shakespeare's familiarity with Roman authors and Roman narratives by 1608 was of the sort that comes only after years of reading and writing on the subject, of watching other plays on the Romans. What distinguishes the Roman tragedies of Shakespeare from a *Hamlet* or a *Lear,* claims Vivian Thomas, is that "[t]he Roman plays are history plays and political plays as well as tragedies. . . . They can be called tragedies, but they constitute a special kind of tragedy—a unique blend of history, politics, and tragic fall. Unless this mixture is appreciated, and savoured, critics and theatergoers will be unduly perplexed and disappointed" (8). Thomas's observations are astute. Attempting a critical reading of *Coriolanus* as a single kind of tragedy is of little benefit if readers are unaware of Shakespeare's conception of Rome, which makes Shakespeare's use of North's Plutarch as a primary source for his drama on Caius Martius significant. Plutarch's narratives are often more biographical than historical, showing what was great or awful about Antony, Cleopatra, Martius, and others, rich material for Shakespeare's vision of tragedies culled from historiographical sources. Jaques Amyot, whose French translation of Plutarch Thomas North first translated into English 1579, wrote a preface to his work that spells out for readers the rewards of historical narratives:

> History is a certain rule and instruction, which by examples past, teacheth us to judge of things present, and to foresee things to come, so as we may know what to like of, and what to follow; what to mislike, and what to eschew. It is a picture . . . setteth before our eyes the things worthy of remembrance that have been done in old times by mighty nations, noble kings and princes, wise governors, valiant captains, and persons renowned for some notable quality, representing unto us the manners of strange nations, the laws, and customs, of old time, the particular affairs of men, their consultations and enterprises, the means that they have used to compass them withal, and their demeaning of themselves when they were come to the highest, or thrown down to the lowest degree of state.[38]

For Shakespeare and his contemporaries, that history was didactic was an oft-repeated precept. Great historical figures who fell from heights of happiness were excellent models for tragedy, a genre considered by Sidney to be didactic in its own right. Renowned historical figures provided, as Amyot argues, "examples," which are "the very forms of our deeds," not just abstractions, such as moral philosophers forward.[39] Acted out upon a stage, these examples undoubtedly made moving arguments for moral behaviors, however they were received. From Plutarch, Shakespeare developed dramas from a broad span of time, one that allowed audiences to see the successes and failures of a developing and developed empire. The republic that Martius struggled in was not the empire that Antony battled against.[40] Caius Martius lived centuries before Antony.[41] The rich diet of examples provided by Plutarch provided Shakespeare with the combination of moral and historical material that was as intellectually engaging as it was controversial.

Plutarch's biography of Caius Martius Coriolanus begins not on the note of conflict that we see in the opening lines of Shakespeare's *Coriolanus*, but almost at the beginning, as it were, of Caius Martius's life. That Caius Martius was from a noble Roman family yet virtuous despite the early loss of his father is related.[42] Caius Martius is a great soldier, devoted to state and family, embodying fully the Roman virtue of *pietas*, respect for the gods, for the family, and for the state, all three of which the Roman put before personal desire or needs.[43] Plutarch tells us that Martius's one flaw was his personality, or lack of. Martius was a disagreeable person; his manner was too "stern" for most. Plutarch notes that had Martius been educated, as we presume he was not in any but the martial arts, he might have learned how to interact well with others. Plutarch writes:

> For this *Martius* naturall wit and great harte dyd marvelously sturre up his corage, to doe and attempt notable actes. But on the other side for lacke of education, he was so chollericke and impacient, that he would yeld to no living creature: which made him churlishe, uncivill, and altogether unfit for any mans conversation. (Brockbank 314)

From this short description we see the Caius Martius Coriolanus of Shakespeare: the short-tempered, glib, exacting, and severe Roman soldier.

Shakespeare's Martius is not Plutarch's, however, nor are other key characters, such as Volumnia, Aufidias, and Menenius. Shakespeare's practice had always been to make liberal and free use of primary sources, but at the same time to recontextualize the borrowed material, or to suppress or exploit material available, making original what was not originally his own. Reading a primary source as one means to interpreting Shakespeare's plays is thus useful in terms of understanding one perspective on a character's historical background or the ideological stance of the author and Shakespeare's departure from both.

From Plutarch, Shakespeare took Caius Martius Coriolanus, son, husband, father of a young son, devoted to Roman values and ideals, especially martial ones, like *virtus*.[44] Successful in wars, Shakespeare's Martius expected others to fight as valiantly for Rome as he did; his taking of the city of Corioles won him a surname, and also a chance at being a consul in the senate. He was turned down by the people for the consulate, as they sensed his lack of sympathy for their hunger and want of corn. Two other men were chosen instead. The rejection irritated him. His speech against the "insolence" of the people in the senate during a meeting over how a shipment of corn was to be dispersed, as well as his suggestion that the tribuneships be abolished, led to the tribunes' leaving the senate and stirring the people against Martius. After a few angry meetings between Martius and the people (stirred into a rage by the tribunes), Martius was banished. Out of revenge for the banishment, Martius turned to Tullus Aufidias, his most hated enemy, and offered his military services to wage war on Rome. Successful as a leader of Aufidias's men, Martius incurs the envy of Aufidias. Martius prepares to attack Rome, yet is petitioned by his mother not to attack the city. Martius capitulates. Seeing Martius vulnerable, an envious Aufidias has him assassinated in the marketplace of Corioles.

That is Plutarch's version, in brief. Shakespeare made several modifications. Shakespeare enlarged the characters of Aufidias, Menenius, and Volumnia, developing each as individuals who play critical roles in Martius's perception of himself as a Roman, a warrior, a father, husband, son: a man. Those three characters are mentioned in Plutarch only as they relate to the story of Martius's rise and fall. For Shakespeare, all three also reveal the hypocrisies and contradictions of Roman warrior culture to which Martius affixes so much importance: valor, honor, and fidelity to state. To fight for Rome, to bring glory to the Roman state is what Martius idealizes. Shakespeare's Volumnia not only petitions her son not to destroy Rome (Brockbank 361–63), but Shakespeare also adds her urging Martius to acquiesce to the tribunes so that Martius may have the consulate, an important moment in the play. This is not in Plutarch, for the question of the consulate was not at issue regarding his banishment. Shakespeare's Volumnia brags mightily to her daughter-in-law Virgilia about having transferred to Martius those virtues necessary to being a great Roman warrior and tells Martius that he must be more solicitous with the tribunes if he is to rise to political greatness. Martius feels that any appeal to the tribunes would compromise his values, his very being. He cannot understand what his mother asks of him, as she is the woman who has instilled in him those Roman virtues with which he honors Rome and their family name. Also in Shakespeare, it is clear that Martius needs continuously to prove himself worthy of Roman honor as a means to finding approval from his mother. In Plutarch's version, Martius is no more than respectful of his mother's wishes that he not sack Rome. In no way do we see in Plutarch's version the dominating mother, Shakespeare's Volumnia, whom Shakespeare creates possibly to provide a key to Martius's response to social values and traditions.

Whereas Plutarch blames a lack of education on Martius's lack of political adeptness (Brockbank 314), Shakespeare instead surrounds the short-tempered Martius with those whose perception of honor falls short of his perception. In turn, Martius does not appear boorish so much as naïve about his idealized perception of Rome and his role in affirming that perception. Martius's sense of honor is rooted in an ideal of Roman *virtus*, which he fulfills through his military exploits. Besides being a good soldier, he honors his family, although family admittedly comes second to state in Rome. He mouths values such as honor and glory, he acts on them, yet he little grasps the responsibility one must take for his actions. He claims glory not for himself but for Rome, yet he little considers the plebeians as being Roman, as being part of the social order he claims to support. Shakespeare's Martius calls the people "curs," "fragments," "inconstant," and "hares," but not "lions," a character trait Martius would have the Roman man bearing. To Martius, a man not fighting for Rome and displaying strength, courage, and fidelity to the state was not worthy of being a Roman. And if a man were not Roman, he was not a man, not a whole person; he was a fragment of the Roman corps, a beast.

Another character who is not developed in Plutarch but is much developed in Shakespeare is Tullus Aufidias. A "lion / that I am proud to hunt" (1.1.233) is what Shakespeare's Martius names Tullus Aufidias, a foe to Rome, as he sees in his enemy his match at martial prowess. Aufidias is mentioned early in the play, in a vision by Martius of what a real soldier embodies, a soldier who would allow Martius to test his mettle, to show all his greatness at fighting. Since what makes Rome great is its warriors, at least in Martius's mind, and their ability to dominate those who fight against them, Martius needs a match in martial prowess to increase the honors. Martius mistakenly believes Aufidias is of the same mind; again, Shakespeare presents a Martius who creates a reality so over-idealized that he falls victim to it: ambitious people are opportunists, too, not just idealists. Aufidias's part in Plutarch, on the other hand, is minimal.

Menenius is little mentioned in Plutarch, too, though he is much developed in Shakespeare. As he does in Plutarch, Menenius tells the people the tale of the belly to discourage a rebellion. Shakespeare's Menenius is a patrician, trusted by both patricians and plebeians, which we do not see in Plutarch. Martius's refusal to hear Menenius's plea for Rome when he visits the enemy Volscian camp is a singularly important moment in

Shakespeare's play, but it does not appear in Plutarch, who only says that groups of friends, relatives, and priests twice visit Martius to petition him not to sack their city. Menenius is not mentioned as one. In Shakespeare, Menenius is a self-described moderate, who feels almost a father to the fatherless Martius. Watching Menenius turned away from Martius's camp and humiliated by his own bragging of how Martius would welcome him, an audience sees the great difficulty that burdens society when political moderates and idealists clash, an idea not expressed in Plutarch.

Besides enlarging historical figures, Shakespeare suppressed information related by Plutarch. As Plutarch tells it, the Rome of Caius Martius Coriolanus, while a republic, embodied two classes or ranks of people at odds with one another: the patricians, or the wealthy, and the plebeians, or the underclass (whom North translates as the people). During this time in Martius's life "there grewe sedition in the cittie, bicause the Senate dyd favour the riche against the people, who dyd complaine of the sore oppression of userers, of whom they borrowed money" (Brockbank 318). Those who failed to pay back their loans either lost their property or were made "bondsmen" to creditors, even those who had fought in previous wars and had the scars to prove it. Worse, the senators had promised the citizens who had fought in a recent war against the *Sabynes* that they "would intreate them more gently" (Brockbank 318), but they ignored the pleas of the citizens for assistance against the usurers. The citizens rebelled, which in turn led some of Rome's enemies to take advantage of the city's vulnerable state. Roman lands outside the city were destroyed, leading the city officials to institute a mandatory draft into military service; the citizens refused (Brockbank 319). Some members of the senate began to question whether or not they should succor the plebeians; Martius was not sympathetic to them, claiming that the rebellion was "prowde attempt of the communaltie . . . to abolish lawe, and to bring all to confusion" (Brockbank 319). The rebels left the city and sat in silent protest on a nearby hill (Brockbank 319). The senate then took action: they sent Menenius Agrippa and others to plead with the citizens to return. Plutarch's Menenius tells the plebeians the tale of the belly and convinces them to return to Rome, allowing them representation by two tribunes who, in fact, had stirred the plebeians into rebellion, Sicinius Vellutus and Junius Brutus (Brockbank 320).

Satisfied, the plebeians, or people, went to war for Rome, hoping, according to Plutarch, that it would be to their advantage. Martius, who valued soldiership, sensed that the patricians would have to raise their estimation in the eyes of the people by fighting, so they did (Brockbank

321). It was in this battle against the Corioles that Martius distinguished himself as a soldier, taking Corioles after he chased its fleeing soldiers to the city gates. Caught up in the retreating rush of men, he found himself inside, with few Romans nearby (Brockbank 322). In what Plutarch describes as "wonderfull [sic]" and "incredible," Martius began single-handedly to attack the enemy soldiers, who fled or dropped their weapons (Brockbank 322). Plutarch does not say that the confusion among the retreating soldiers was probably as much assistance to Martius as his juggernaut manner; at any rate, another Roman soldier managed to let more Romans in the gates, and the city was Rome's. Shakespeare does not mention that Caius Martius was carried into the gates with other Volscians retreating to their city; instead, he shows Martius alone entering the gates and Martius alone fighting. In Plutarch, it appears that Lartius Titus, another great soldier, and perhaps a few other Romans made it into the city gates, too. That Martius enters alone in Shakespeare's play is crucial to Martius's sense of identity and to one of the play's greatest ironies: the title that distinguished Martius from other Romans also earned him the surname Coriolanus.[45] It is the single most distinguished act in Martius's military career. After that, Martius never rises to a greater position in the Roman state. It appears Shakespeare wanted to show Martius as a figure of superhuman strength and will, someone closer to the divine than the average Roman. This has the effect of creating a greater distance between Martius and the people. The more godlike Caius Martius looks, the more unworthy look the people.

Shakespeare does not mention the complaints of usury and bondage or the rebels' quiet protest. He also does not mention the scars that the people earned in wars. Shakespeare begins his play with the citizens rebelling over corn prices and Menenius offering the tale of the belly as a means to convince them not to resort to violence. Plutarch does, in fact, mention the plebeians' complaints over corn prices, but that occurs after Corioles is taken and after the senate has ignored the military service proffered by the people—for the second time. Thus, while Martius's reputation with the senate and patricians was secured, it meant little to a people whose efforts in the war did not win them peacetime favor with the senate. Participation in the wars left fields untilled and unplanted; a corn dearth set in. The tribunes convinced the people that enough corn was not available, stirring them once again to sedition, as Plutarch notes (Brockbank 328). To prevent concern over lack of grain and to rid Rome of troublemakers, the senate voted to send some of the rebels to a local community, Velitres, which had lost much of its citizenry to a plague and had asked that Romans move in to help repopulate the community. The rest were to be sent to war against the Volces; it was also hoped that the patricians and plebeians fighting together would create mutual respect between the two groups (Brockbank 329). Neither idea appealed to Sicinius and Brutus, the tribunes, who urged the people to ignore the orders to leave. Martius, at this point, "openely spake against these flattering Tribunes" (Brockbank 330) and demanded the people follow commands of the government. The people refused. In response, Martius, with a few men, headed to a region belonging to the Antiates and took corn, cattle, and men into bondage. These he brought back to Rome, the spoils being shown to go to those who were willing to fight (Brockbank 330). Martius's willingness to put Rome before himself earned him the right to a consul seat, which had to be approved by the people. Highly disliked, Martius nevertheless earns grudging respect for his devotion to Rome, but not for long.

Shakespeare cuts the anecdote about Velitres from his translation of Plutarch to the stage. Shakespeare makes no mention of moving citizens to another city, which shows how little control they had over their lives, or of Martius's foray into Antiate land, which shows his aggressive nature. Plutarch's version makes the citizens more sympathetic, the Shakespeare's, the Roman warrior less godlike. Clearer in Plutarch than in Shakespeare, however, is that the tribunes are responsible for the sedition and poor relationship between patricians and plebeians. To be sure, the tribunes come off badly in Shakespeare, but Martius's attacks upon their character seem generated by his disgust with their holding positions of power, not with their abuses of that power.[46] In both Plutarch and Shakespeare, the tribunes are key to Martius's banishment, to his changing fortune, for even if Plutarch shows Martius's unpleasant manner as a flaw in character, his deeds spoke for themselves to both the patricians and the plebeians: it was the tribunes who encouraged the people to reject Martius's consulship, which in turn led to a series of circumstances that change Martius's fortunes for the worse. Martius felt betrayal at such a personal level that the tribunes look like Judases.

To be elected to consul, Martius needed not only the support of politicians and patricians but also the approval of the people. Plutarch relates how it was tradition for a candidate to appear in the marketplace for a few days, humbly appareled, to entreat the common people's voice for the desired office. The showing of wounds and the willingness to wear coarse clothing showed humility, not to mention service to Rome.

Plutarch writes that "*Martius* following this custome, shewed many woundes and cuttes apon his bodie, which he had received in seventeene yeres service at the warres, and in many sundrie battells" (Brockbank 332), indicating Martius Caius's willingness to show himself worthy of service to Rome in a capacity other than soldier, even if he was rude-tongued. Shakespeare, however, does not characterize Martius this way. Shakespeare's Martius refuses to bare his wounds and scars to the common people, although he does wear the modest gown. Shakespeare's reason for not presenting a Martius who shows a willingness to win the goodwill of the plebeians cannot be known, of course, but his doing so seems to support a direction in which he wishes to take the audience.

Martius's refusal to expose himself is a visual of a theme Shakespeare sounds throughout the play: Martius's fear of exposing his vulnerability. The wounds and scars show Martius to be mortal, permeable, and penetrable, conditions which he refuses to acknowledge in himself. As a Roman, Martius has come to believe in the Roman mythos of *pietas*, but at the same time he cannot stand that being Roman includes plebeians and other common folk. When Martius rants at the plebeians, he shows contempt not only for them, but also for Rome and in turn for himself, for the veneer of Roman with which he has covered himself. This is evident in Shakespeare's having Martius not only mock the tradition of not standing before the people, but also mock the common people who come to question him in the marketplace. After he has asked for the voice of one group of citizens, alone, Shakespeare's Martius wonders,

> Better it is to die, better to starve,
> Than crave the hire which first we do deserve.
> Why in this wolvish toge should I stand here,
> To beg of Hob and Dick that does appear
> Their needless vouches? Custom calls me to't.
> What custom wills, in all things should we do't,
> The dust on antique time would lie unswept
> And mountainous error be too highly heap'd
> For truth to o'erpeer. Rather than fool it so,
> Let the high office and the honour go
> To one that would do thus. (2.3.113–22)

Martius's short monologue is telling: he believes that by virtue of being a great warrior, he deserves the office of consul, and that the voices of the plebeians, the "Hobs" and "Dicks" (English common names) are without value; "needless," he calls them. Miserable in his modest "toge," Martius ponders the Roman custom of begging for voices, yet he notes with irony how custom comes before truth. Martius is a traditionalist. That he agrees to go through the motions indicates his great devotion to Rome, albeit an abstraction.[47] Ironically, though, he fails to see what he values as being custom, too. When custom suits him, he yields without question. At this point in the play, we begin to sense that Martius does what he does because it is expected of him. He closes his monologue with the resolve that he was "half through, / the one part suffer'd, the other will [he] do" (2.3.122–23).

In Shakespeare's version of Martius, the young Roman has become a great soldier not so much for himself but for another, for his mother. Volumnia plays a relatively small part in Plutarch's biography, but in Shakespeare's play she dominates, as we learn from her, from Menenius, and from other Romans. Shakespeare's Volumnia dreams to have as much honor given the family name as her son can earn her. One way to gain honor was through election to the consul seat. Thus, when Volumnia heard that her son took Corioles and would stand for consul, she told Menenius that he took wounds in the shoulder and in the left arm and that "there will be large cicatrices to show the people when he shall stand for his place" (2.1.146–48). Volumnia, before she has even seen her son return from Corioles in triumph, presumes Martius would want to show his scars to the people as a matter of course in his rise to consul. It does not occur to her that her son would not follow tradition. When she sees Martius upon his return from Corioles, she tells him

> I have liv'd
> To see inherited my very wishes,
> And the buildings of my fancy: only
> There's one thing wanting, which I doubt not but
> Our Rome will cast upon thee. (2.1.197–200)

We know Volumnia's fancy, but not that of Martius. Martius has followed, apparently without reflection, the course set by his mother, and it has brought him the fame and the honor she desires. What Volumnia did not know was that she also instilled in him a patrician disgust of the lower classes of Rome that is reflected in his puerile arrogance toward them in the marketplace. Martius may have won his first battle at sixteen, but after many wars, a marriage, and a child, he is no more a man psychologically, socially, or emotionally than a youth is an adult. Taunted by the tribunes, who announce that the people did not give their voice for his consulship, Martius easily succumbs to name-calling and character assassination. To be sure, the tribunes, fearing Martius would fight to end the tribune position if he were a consul, work hard to agitate the people against him. Their self-interest fails to earn audience sympathy, so that when Martius rants at them, what he says about them is not untrue. The problem is that Martius makes it too evident that he regards himself as being of superior rank, saying to the senators of the people:

> In soothing them, we nourish 'gainst our senate
> The cockle of rebellion, insolence, sedition,
> Which we ourselves have plough'd for, sow'd and scatter'd,
> By mingling them with us, the honour'd number
> Who lack not virtue, no, more power, but that
> Which they have given to beggars. (3.1.68–73)

Martius believes himself to be of an "honoured number," as probably did others born into the aristocratic ranks who maintained power by oppressing those born in nonaristocratic ranks, convincing them they deserved no more than they had. Martius tells the truth about life in "republican" Rome, and it is offensive to the hearers, for different reasons. Those who wish Martius would learn to control his temper around the tribunes and people find his manner offensive, not the political truths about Roman aristocracy. And while the senators probably do not care to give the people representation, they do fear rebellion. Martius adamantly opposes representation, seeing it as one step toward equality among all Romans. He does not want to be like the people, for his mother has raised him to loathe them. When she comes to petition Martius to ameliorate the tribunes, to wear his bonnet and coarse gown before them, Martius seems confused. To Volumnia he says,

> I muse my mother
> Does not approve me further, who was wont
> To call them woolen vassals, things created
> To buy and sell with groats, to show bare heads
> In congregations, to yawn, be still, and wonder,
> When one but of my ordinance stood up
> To speak of peace or war. (3.2.8–13)

Martius's arrogant self-righteousness about granting representation to the people makes sense in light of how he was raised. His mother has nurtured in him a sense of self that is defined as much by what he is as by what he is not. He is not a plebeian, he is a patrician. Plebeians are dull and inconstant, easily bought and sold, metaphorically speaking. They are things. Martius does not associate plebeians with the Romans for whom he fights or the Rome to which he brings glory and war treasure. He is so elitist and narrow-minded that it never seems to occur to him that plebeians are Romans, just as he is a Roman. Thus, he really fights for only a small number of Romans, the senators and patricians, in his own mind. Yet after he is banished, all Romans are Romans except for Caius Martius.

NOTES

1. Andrew Gurr, *The Shakespearean Stage*, 3rd Ed. (Cambridge, England: Cambridge UP, 1992), p. 117, distinguishes hall playhouses, like the Theater, from amphitheater playhouses, like the Globe. The Theater, built by James Burbage in 1576, soon found competition in other hall playhouses, such as the Curtain, which opened a year later, and the Rose, which opened in 1587.

2. Glynn Wickam et al., *Theatre in Europe: A Documentary History: English Professional Theatre, 1530–1660* (Cambridge, England: Cambridge UP, 2000), p. 295, notes that four inns operated as playing places beginning in the 1570s through the 1590s, when they were finally banned from allowing plays at the insistence of London magistrates—the Bel Savage, the Bull, the Cross Keys, and the Bell.

3. Ibid., pp. 17–19.

4. Ibid., pp. 33–47, cites a number of records, which show the anxiety felt by the ruling order over the power of theatrical performances to stir social unrest

5. Gurr, *Shakespearean Stage*, p. 27, cites the 1572 Acte for the punishment of Vacabondes, which names players of interludes, among other itinerant tradesmen, as needing permission to peddle goods. The idea, it seems, was to control mobility of persons in the realm and subsequently to ensure that those who tied themselves to a community would be assured of earning money from their trade with less competition from others. Wickham, *Theatre in Europe*, pp. 33–47, writes that vagabond laws were enacted in 1563, 1572, 1576, and 1584–1585, mostly as a response to the rising number of theater groups.

6. Licenses for performances were required as early as 1559. T. W. Baldwin, *The Organization and Personnel of the Shakespearean Company* (Princeton, NJ: Princeton UP, 1927) p. 12, writes that in 1574, the Earl of Leicester granted a company a "patent" securing for them the right to perform in London and other places in England, except where other laws or patents superseded.

7. Ibid., p. 35.

8. Ibid., p. 38.

9. Apprentices usually worked under a master for eleven years before they could graduate to a master (Baldwin, *Shakespearean Company*, p. 285).

10. Ibid., p. 287, conjectures Shakespeare joined the company that became known as the Lord Chamberlain's Men around 1588 as an apprentice or hired man, and that by 1594, he was a member. Because of the paucity of records on Shakespeare's life or his acting career, conjecture must serve.

11. On May 19, 1603, a patent was issued, bestowing upon Shakespeare's company the title of the King's Men, which in turn made them "His Majesty's Servants," a prestigious designation for the actors not granted any other. S. Schoenbaum, *Shakespeare, The Globe, and the World* (Oxford: Oxford UP, 1979), p. 125.

12. Baldwin, *Shakespearean Company*, p. 68.

13. Outside London, other licensed companies were operating (Baldwin, *Shakespearean Company*, p. 285), but for this study only the London companies are of importance.

14. In an anonymous poem printed 1619, "A Funeral Elegy on the Death of the famous Actor Richard Burbage . . ." is written the following: "No more, young Hamlet, old Hieronimo, / Kind Lear, the grieved Moor, and more beside, / That liv'd in him, have now forever died" (Rpt. in Wickham et al., *Theatre in Europe*, p. 182).

15. Baldwin, *Shakespearean Company*, pp. 314–15.

16. Amphitheaters held more people, with the Globe holding a minimum of 3,000. By comparison, the first and second Blackfriars held fewer than 600; after 1608 when Shakespeare owned both, his company profited more from Blackfriars (Gurr, *Shakespearean Stage*, p. 117).

17. Geoffrey Bullough, ed., *Narrative and Dramatic Sources of Shakespeare, V: The Roman Plays*, 8 vols. (London: Routledge, 1964), 5:496. Florus, another historian, refers to Coriolanus during the reign of Hadrian, according to Michael D. Bristol, "Lenten Butchery: Legitimation Crisis in Coriolanus," in *Shakespeare Reproduced: The Text in History and Ideology*, ed. Jean E. Howard and Marion F. O'Connor (New York: Methuen, 1987), p. 473. Around 1600, a French play, *Coriolan*, was in circulation. A Senecan-style tragedy, it was written by Alexandre Hardy, but it is doubtful Shakespeare knew it (Ibid., p. 474).

18. Coppélia Kahn, *Roman Shakespeare: Warriors, Wounds, and Women* (New York: Routledge, 1997), p. 11, cites Clifford Ronan's study, *Antike Roman: Power Symbology and the Roman Play in Early Modern England, 1585–1635* (Athens: University of Georgia Press, 1995), pointing out that Roman plays set in Rome would number 31. Between 1608 and 1612, encompassing the time *Coriolanus* was thought to be written, five extant Roman plays were written in London, making up in some years a relatively high percentage. In 1612, only three plays are extant, and one was Roman in theme, says Ronan, p. 185.

19. Bullough, *Narrative and Dramatic Sources*, p. 25, claims that until *Julius Caesar*, extant Roman plays were closet dramas, those written for recitation (but not for the stage) by Lady Pembroke and her acquaintances, suggesting that "[i]n

writing *Julius Caesar*, Shakespeare may well have been the initiator of a fashion in the popular theater."

20. In a prefatory note, "To the Readers," in *Sejanus, His Fall in Ben Jonson: Five Plays*, ed. and intro. G. A. Wilkes (Oxford: Oxford UP, 1981), Jonson defends his work as being what he considers a true "poem" or "dramatic poem," based upon precepts he has exacted from Horace's *Art of Poetry*, a text he was translating. Jonson writes, "in truth of argument, dignity of persons, gravity and height of elocution, fullness, and frequency of sentence, I have discharged the office of tragic writer" (pp. 103–04). Jonson wants the reader to believe that he has written a historically accurate poem on a noble figure in elevated language. Jonson concedes, however, that he has not followed the "strict rules of time," nor has he included a chorus (104).

21. As early as 55 B.C., Julius Caesar began raids in England, prior to the Roman occupation, according to Graham Webster, *The Roman Invasion of Britain* (New York: Routledge, 1999), p. 36.

22. English translations: on Tacitus was Sir Henry Savile's *Histories* 1591 and Richard Greneway's *Annals* 1598; Philemon Holland's Livy was available in 1600. Kahn, *Roman Shakespeare*, pp. 9–10, holds that Shakespeare still had a number of cultural sources for Roman-ness when he began writing his Roman plays in 1590, as English versions of Roman history and legends were in circulation for centuries.

23. Robert Miola, *Shakespeare's Rome* (Cambridge, England: Cambridge UP, 1983), p. 17. Vergil (Publius Vergilius Maro, 70–19 B.C.) wrote the *Aeneid*, a fictional account of the founding of Rome by the Trojan, Aeneas.

24. Ronan, *Antike Roman*, p. 3, says these virtues were stereotypical, but often lacking in the Roman characters found on stage.

25. Lily B. Campbell, *Shakespeare's Tragic Heroes* (New York: Barnes and Noble, 1952), p. 15.

26. Timothy Hampton, *Writing from History: The Rhetoric of Exemplarity in Renaissance Literature* (Ithaca: Cornell UP, 1990) p. 15, claims that for the Italian humanists, "[t]he rediscovery of and return to the texts of Roman culture coincided with the rise of the Italian city-state, where social structure required an educated elite able to read and write good administrative Latin. The obvious stylistic models for Latin instruction were Roman."

27. Literally, *de casibus virorum illustrium* can be translated as "fall of great men," or the fate of great people, brought low by Fortune, or fate, not necessarily by their own doing.

28. Paul Budra, *A Mirror for Magistrates and the de casibus Tradition* (Toronto: U of Toronto P, 2000), p. 15.

29. Iser, p. 41.

30. Emrys Jones, *The Origins of Shakespeare* (Oxford: Oxford UP, 1977), pp. 46–47.

31. D. F. Bratchell, ed. *Shakespearean Tragedy* (New York: Routledge, 1952),

p. 4. Ibid., pp. 7–8, also claims that until the Restoration, Shakespeare's works were judged by Restoration neoclassicists, who found his plays faulty for ignoring the unities or other "ideals" of tragedy.

32. Aristotle himself refers us to his "published works" in the *Poetics*, more evidence of a lost body of work, p. 25.

33. As Jones, *Origins*, reminds us, neoclassicism begins for England in the early sixteenth century with Erasmus (1466–1536), who translated texts from Greek to Latin, making some Greek works available for study. Latin was a staple in the grammar school classroom, where boys were familiarized with Roman literature in translation exercises, among others (pp. 6–13). Thus, there is a neoclassic sensibility in the Renaissance and the Restoration, but the degree to which writers in either period were influenced differs. Shakespeare seems to have been familiar with Greek ideas about drama as they were interpreted through translations, but that he was disposed to strictly adhering to particular neoclassical dramatic practices seems not the case.

34. Anne Barton, "Livy, Machiavelli, and Shakespeare's Coriolanus," *Shakespeare Survey* 38 (1985), p. 116, cites lines 134 to 139 in Menenius's tale of the belly, which explain "the distribution of nourishment through the blood, derive from Livy's, not Plutarch's, version."

35. According to Miola, *Shakespeare's Rome*, p. 11, the fable of the belly as told by Menenius is a "composite of passages" from the following Roman sources, in addition to Plutarch and Livy: William Avery's *A Mervaillous Combat of Contrarieties* (1588), William Camden's *Remaines* (1605), Philip Sidney's *Apology* (1595), and perhaps, but not certainly, Camerarius's *Fabellae Aesopicae* (1579).

36. Anne Barton, "Livy," p. 116.

37. Ibid., p. 116, explains that Livy was a historian of the city of Rome and its inhabitants; Miola, in *Shakespeare's Rome*, p. 4, writes that Plutarch was a "moral and anecdotal historian."

38. Rubin Headlam Wells, *Shakespeare, Politics, and the State* (London: Macmillan, 1986), pp. 133–34.

39. Ibid., p. 134.

40. For another perspective, see Paul Cantor's *Shakespeare's Rome: Republic and Empire* (Ithaca: Cornell UP, 1976) for an analysis of Shakespeare's development of character from his notion of Roman-ness.

41. According to Bullough, *Narrative and Dramatic Sources*, p. 464, Plutarch's source for Caius Marcus was Dionysius of Halicarnassus (c. 66 B.C.–c. A.D. 10), who wrote the twenty-nine books *Roman Antiquities* in Greek when he came to Rome about 29 B.C. In Book Six was the story of Rome, 491 B.C., Menennius, and Gnaeus Marcius (Caius Martius), who is regarded as responsible for taking Corioli, for being "sober and restrained in his private life," and for taking only a horse and one captive, for which he earned respect.

42. Philip Brockbank, ed., *Coriolanus. The Arden Shakespeare* (London:

Methuen, 1976), pp. 313–14. All citations for Plutarch are from this work by Brockbank.

43. Wells, *Shakespeare, Politics, and the State*, pp. 110–11.

44. Plutarch says that *virtus* in Latin meant "valliantness" (Brockbank, *Coriolanus*, p. 314).

45. Ibid., p. 327, describes the surname as a third name given to those who were marked by a physical characteristic or personal trait. He also adds that the name was given to ancient Greek "Princes" when they performed a special feat or deed.

46. I should note here that not all agree that the tribunes come off badly. Ralph Berry in *Shakespeare and Social Class* (Atlantic Highlands, NJ: Humanities Press International, 1988), p. 151, thinks that the tribunes are "thoroughgoing professionals," elected officials who do the job expected of them—to mediate between the patricians and plebeians. When they plot to rid Rome of Martius, however, I think that they breach their professional duties.

47. Miola in *Shakespeare's Rome* thinks that for Shakespeare, Rome "maintained a "distinct identity," that it had a "palpable though ever-changing presence," p. 17. This Rome is like Martius's Rome, not so much a place as an idea, indeed the idea of Rome that so many authors helped foster in the tradition that he inherited.

3

DRAMATIC STRUCTURE

The dramatic structure of *Coriolanus* shows Shakespeare's mastery of heroic characterization and current vogues in tragic form. Disciplined in its language and plot structure, the play has what Maurice Charney called a "lean vigor."[1] Martius's lines are terse, wrought with a tension that surfaces at the hero's every expression. Although Coriolanus has been perceived as a character who lacks inwardness and thus fails to appeal to his audience the way that a Lear or Hamlet does, the fact is, Caius Martius in word and deed says as much, if not more, about himself than a character who tells us what to think. Martius's tragedy is that of a man who sees himself as living the ideal of Roman *virtus*, but who fails to understand the compromise that must be made between ideal and practice if one is to live easily with others in a social order.

A virtuous, unselfish, devoted servant to the state of Rome, Coriolanus honors country and family. Yet Coriolanus never feels peace. Even when he is at the zenith of his career, he cannot experience a conflict-free moment. The lack of quiet in Coriolanus's psychological and emotional make-up is echoed in the play's battery of discordant noises. Marching soldiers, clashing swords, beating drums, blasting horns, and shouting mobs intrude from the play's start. A persistent tension is created by the many adversarial relationships between Caius Martius and the plebeians, soldiers at Corioles, Aufidias, his mother, or the tribunes. As the plot unfolds, the enigma that is Coriolanus is exposed. By the play's end, we find a man who never discovers himself, whose identity is entirely shaped by a fantastic vision of Roman-ness, passed on to him by his mother. The human inside Martius is repressed. When he is banished from the culture that shaped and nourished him, he looks for his identity in another soldier, Aufidias, and finds there a mockery of his ideal.

Shakespeare exposes the hypocrisy of Roman ideals in a number of ways through his hero. In short, the ideal is destructive to self and society. It relies on an aristocratic elitism that serves the few at the cost of many. Even the heroes in such a system are used. A patrician, Caius Martius is born into the class that allows him to live the Roman ideal that his mother fantasizes for him. He has opportunities. He views himself as superior to the plebeians and therefore is not inclined to share with them what he feels he has earned through military service. Martius does not have to till fields or work a trade or keep a house to survive. He does not have to leave fields untilled to fight a battle against Roman enemies. He is less likely to be affected by a grain dearth or the economics of distribution. When the hungry plebeians rebel, Martius is unsympathetic. He feels that he works hard, which explains his success and lack of hunger, seeing the opposite as true of the plebeians. Thus, the senate's giving the plebeians representation, allowing them tribunes, infuriates him. For him, it marks a paradigm shift in Roman politics that he wishes to subvert. He revisits the theme of representation throughout the play, as it comes to stand for control, for power, for voice. Caius Martius naively believes that his voice, his place in society, supersedes other voices, almost as if it were granted by divine right. He never regards himself as "used" by the state, represented by the senate, his mother, or Menenius. Naturally, he sees those who are not his equal as using him: the tribunes and the plebeians. They do not mirror for him the virtues that he values, and thus are suspect. One by one, those whom Martius most admires let him down.

Although it is the plebeians having representation against which Coriolanus most consistently rails, it is Coriolanus's vulnerability as a human being against which he struggles.[2] The plebeians represent to him the vulnerability implicit in being human, and it is that dependent state of humans upon the most basic of needs, nourishment, to which the audience's attention is first drawn. The play opens with a band of mutiny-minded citizens armed with "staves, clubs, and other weapons." First Citizen opens the play with the lines, "Before we proceed any further, hear me speak," or in other words, "listen to me," an immediate appeal to the audience and a signal that the citizens have something important to communicate. The audience is immediately drawn into the conflict facing the citizens, not that of the hero. First Citizen asks his compatriots if they are all in agreement regarding their uprising, that they "are all resolved to die than to famish" (3–4). All humans need food to survive. Their mortal states require it. What responsibilities members of a society have to themselves as a group and as individuals figure strongly as a theme in this play, but it is the tragic hero who represents most frighteningly the fragility of the mortal state and its reliance on similarly fragile humans. Coriolanus attempts to escape that fragility but cannot, any more than he can escape his Roman peers. Instead of facing the fact that the citizens are hungry from the grain dearth (and that he, like them, is equally vulnerable to hunger), Martius insults them and mocks their right to voice their troubles. In his first appearance in the play, Caius Martius briefly greets Menenius, who is calming the rebel citizens, then he rudely turns to the citizens and asks,

> What's the matter, you dissentious rogues
> That, rubbing the poor itch of your opinion,
> Make yourselves scabs? (1.1.163–65)

Martius referencing their "opinion" in a denigrating manner is how the audience is introduced to him, and his opening speech is a "perversion of the traditional speech of war heroes," observes Derek Traversi.[3] Martius does not believe that the citizens deserve an opinion or voice, and he follows with a laundry list of reasons. The people are fickle, "that like not peace nor war" (1.1.168), or they change their minds about whom they admire or dislike according to popular sentiment: "With every minute you do change your mind / And call him noble that was now your hate, / Him vile that as your garland" (1.1.181–83). For Martius, fickleness in the underclass is something to be reviled, especially if it has a voice or representation. The relatively small group of aristocrats and office-holders, who are no doubt as fickle as other humans, pose less of a threat to Martius, for he had friends in both groups. As with most people who prefer that centers of power remain closed and small, Martius wants the control that comes with having the political advantage, not the perceived loss of power (chaos) that results when too many voices threaten to breach an elitist power center.

In this play, references to tongues, mouths, voices,[4] or breaths are often heard. These terms shape the discourse of the play, which addresses an individual's refusal to accept a shift in political power structure, a shift that would compromise his sense of identity. Martius's self has been constructed upon an ideal of Roman-ness that is not as valued as he would wish it. Tongues and mouths, instruments for nourishing ourselves, are closely knit metaphorically with breath and voice. The instruments needed for eating are those needed to communicate will, spirit, feelings, and desires. Voice is the released product of mouth, tongue, breath, and teeth. Shakespeare shows in this play that one of the most intellectual and aesthetically powerful expressions of human emotion, the poetic language of tragedy, relies on the most basic of needs: nourishment. People cannot voice or communicate unless they first have sustenance.

At the same time, Martius shows us a hero who attempts to transcend the need for nourishment to which we are all vulnerable through sheer superhuman strength and will. Coriolanus instead feeds upon the martial ideals perpetuated by the Roman legends and myths, upon the concept of Roman *virtus*. He expresses the ideals that he values in his railings at the plebeians, which perpetuates the idea, but he also uses his mouth and tongue to communicate his frustration at the shift in power structure between the patricians and plebeians. He masks his fear of having to share a voice in the power structure with those whom he sees as less powerful by his sarcastic attitude toward the plebeians. His railings at the plebeians' perceived flaws also affirm the Roman ideals that he feels he embodies. Martius, as Günter Grass notes of him, is unambiguous: he has a "compulsion" to spread what is a truth to himself when he is around the plebeians. Although Grass sees this truth as "scorn, contempt, and hatred" for the plebeians, Martius's contempt is for their newly gained rights to representation. The abstract is what Martius values, not the concrete. When Martius is not true to himself, when he is asked to show more art as a politician by his mother and friends, as Grass points out, he is not being true to himself. When he gives in to his mother, he is false to himself, though he "plays out his part incorrigibly to the end."[5]

Martius's tragic fate is the result not of pride[6] or wrath. His reliance on both stead him well in battle. His actions go beyond pride, even though he presumes his authority and superiority over the plebeians. His is an absurd need to order his existence according to an ideal, a static illusion of what Rome means or is as it relates to his conception of *virtus*.[7] With Caius Martius it is personal, so much so that he bullies the citizens. The great war-hero who fought and brought glory to Rome and his family's name many times mocks the rioters by saying,

> They said they were an-hungry, sigh'd forth proverbs—
> That hunger broke stone walls; that dogs must eat;
> That meat was made for mouths; that the gods sent not
> Corn for the rich men only. With these shreds

> They vented their complainings, which being answer'd
> And a petition granted them, a strange one,
> To break the heart of generosity
> And make bold power look pale, they threw their caps
> As they would hang them on the horns o'th'moon,
> Shouting their emulation. (1.1.204–13)

Martius takes reasonable appeals to traditional values and sources and berates them. In a narrative account of the 1549 Robert Kett uprisings in Norfolk against enclosing farmlands, the poor are said to make a similar argument. First we hear the argument that poor and rich alike both were meant to share in nature's goodness:

> While we (the poor) have the same forme, and the same condition of birth together with them (the rich), why should they have a life so unlike unto ours, and differ so farre from us in calling?[8]

More specifically, the line "hunger broke stone walls" echoes the action threatened by rebelling citizens, to tear down hedges:

> We see now that it is come to extremeties, wee will also proove extremitie: rend downe hedges, fill up ditches, make way for everie man into the common pasture.[9]

Against the reasonable arguments of the citizens, Martius's arguments that the people are cowards or lazy or inconstant are suspect. Martius no doubt feels that his being brave, hard-working, and dutiful to Rome allows him not to have to worry about hunger. In turn, his stereotype of the people affirms what he believes about himself and them. One way to oppress others is to convince them they lack qualities or characteristics that make them more deserving. The fable of the belly told at the play's beginning by Menenius to the seditious citizens implies inferiority on the part of the oppressed and hungry poor. The citizens allow the tale to be told, showing a reasonableness on their part, despite knowing that Menenius is probably going to "fob off [their] disgrace" with a "tale" (1.1.92–93). Menenius begins:

> There was a time, when all the body's members
> Rebell'd against the belly; thus accus'd it:
> That only like a gulf it did remain

I'th'midst o'th'body, idle and unactive,
Still cupboarding the viand, never bearing
Like labour with the rest, where th'other instruments
Did see, and hear, devise, instruct, walk, feel,
And, mutually participate, did minister
Unto the appetite and affection common
Of the whole body. The belly answer'd— (1.1.95–104)

Before Menenius can continue, First Citizen interrupts with "Well, sir, what answer made the belly?" (1.1.105), impatient with the old tale and it relationship to the uprising. Menenius responds,

Sir, I shall tell you. With a kind of smile,
Which ne'er came from the lungs, but even thus—
For look you, I may make the belly smile,
As well as speak—it tauntingly replied
To th'discontented members, the mutinous parts
That envied his receipt; even so most fitly,
As you malign our senators, for that
They are not such as you. (1.1.106–13)

First Citizen interrupts again, more impatient (but still polite) as Menenius has tried to humor the mob with his making his stomach smile, by creasing his stomach or garments or belching, a distraction he hopes will temper their mood. Yet, in turn, he refers to the mob as discontented, mutinous, and envious of the senators. First Citizen, seemingly familiar with the popular early modern analogies of human anatomy to the state, says,

Your belly's answer—what?
The kingly crown'd head, the vigilant eye,
The counsellor heart, the arm our soldier,
Our steed the leg, the tongue our trumpeter,
With other muniments and petty helps
In this our fabric, it that they— (1.1.113–18)

The comment is important to our understanding how politically savvy Shakespeare portrays the plebeians. The corporate analogy introduced by First Citizen, according to Andrew Gurr, was the Aristotelian analogy exploited by Henry Tudor and his heirs. The monarch in the English state was considered a part of the corpus, the head, but like the other members, ruled by the laws of the nation.[10] James I, on the other hand, saw the king as above the law.[11] These plebeians are analogous to English commoners living under the reign of James I, not altogether naive about political power structures, even if Menenius and Martius want us to believe that. Menenius, in fact, has used an analogy that fails, as Krystyna Kujawinski-Courtey argues, because of the decentering of the head to the belly: "Menenius unintentionally dislocates the 'brain' or the 'heart' from their traditionally agreed upon position of command in the human physiological system" (94–95). Menenius becomes perturbed at realizing that his tale has a more sophisticated audience than he had hoped, not to mention one that is aware of a more political rhetoric than he had anticipated. Flustered, Menenius comments on the inversion of social hierarchy and authority when the citizen, a mere plebeian, interrupts the patrician Menenius: "'Fore me this fellow speaks!" (1.1.119). Menenius's prejudice toward the mob is apparent in his own impatience. He presumes his station superior to theirs, and doesn't mind being in their midst, as long as they keep their place. First Citizen, without missing a beat, continues his sentence with "Should by the cormorant belly be restrain'd, / Who is the sink o' th' body—" (1.1.120–21). It is clear at this point that Menenius has failed to impress his audience

The tale is not going the way that Menenius had planned, for Menenius wants to show how the senate is analogous to the stomach. First Citizen has just called the stomach the sink of the body, the senate, thus, being the sink of the community. Menenius, perturbed, says, "Well, what then?" and the quick-witted First Citizen, willing to yield to Menenius his tale, asks as if he is truly interested: "The former agents, if they did complain, / What could the belly answer?" (1.1.122–23). Menenius, being allowed to save face, says, with some degree of graciousness, "I will tell you, / If you'll bestow a small (of what you have little) / Patience awhile, you'st hear the belly's answer" (1.1.123–25). First Citizen, tired of the insults, says, "Y'are long about it" (1.1.126), to which Menenius replies, "Note me this, good friend; / Your most grave belly was deliberate, / Not rash like his accusers" (1.1.126–28).

To this point, there is little to indicate that the mob has been rash or impatient.[12] They are dallied with by Menenius, just as they have been dallied with by the senate. The plebeians are represented by First Citizen, a witty, frank person who knows enough to understand when he is being patronized. For their seditious acts, the plebeians are presumed "rascals," as Menenius calls them, citizens who want much for what little they can offer in return. From his patrician worldview, the plebeians might seem rascals, as their being rascals allows him to patronize them in their low station in life with propagandistic fables. Menenius tells the plebeians in his fable that from the belly, the senators, good comes to them.

> The senators of Rome are this good belly,
> And you the mutinous members: for examine
> Their counsels and their cares, digest things rightly
> Touching the weal o'th'common, you shall find
> No public benefit which you receive
> But it proceeds or comes from them to you,
> And no way from yourselves. (1.1.147–53)

In this passage, we see Menenius's credibility undermined, which anticipates his loss of credibility with Martius later in the play. We also have our attention drawn to the body and its need for nourishment, its need to work as a whole unit to survive. Menenius's tale anatomizes or fragments parts, which speaks to the fragmention of members in Rome's early Republic. The patrimonialism of the hierarchical structure does not allow all members to participate equally, nor does it allow all members equal dignity. Public benefit, whatever that may entail, is received by plebeians because they are in no position to dispense it or dole it out, and if they were, the belief is that they could not be counted on to make moral or ethical decisions about grain dispensation during hard times. Martius claims that the plebeians would "feed upon one another" (1.1.187) if not for the noble senate and its judiciousness.

Martius's appeal to a patrimonial social organization as if it were fostered by the divine is meant to strike at the consciences of seditious citizens, but these citizens have reached a level of need that supersedes tradition and power structure: they are hungry. Martius's appeals seem empty bombast by contrast. The plebeians want affordable grain, not fables or to be told that they are unreliable, inconstant, and cowardly. Yet Martius and Menenius, who are in positions of power, both impose upon the group these characteristics, in their presence. Body parts and beasts are the plebeians to the aristocratic patricians; even worse, Coriolanus calls them "fragments." Zvi Jagendorf says that Coriolanus "imagines himself as complete and self-sufficient," being "positioned between an aristocratic fantasy of wholeness and the despised, fragmented carnal body" (462). Martius's speeches to the plebeians reveal his bias, and the plebeians' responses reveal Martius's ignorance of the plebeian Roman.

Martius, after calling the plebeians rogues, is answered by First Citizen, who says with dripping irony, "We have ever your good word" (1.1.165). Martius answers this truth with a long speech, his "word," on his perspective of the plebeians, and none of it is "good":

> He that will give good words to thee, will flatter
> Beneath abhorring. What would you have, you curs,
> That like nor peace nor war? The one affrights you,
> The other makes you proud. He that trusts to you,
> Where he should find you lions, finds you hares;
> Where foxes, geese: you are no surer, no,
> Than is the coal of fire upon the ice,
> Or hailstone in the sun. Your virtue is,
> To make him worthy whose offence subdues him,
> And curse that justice did it. Who deserves greatness,
> Deserves your hate; and your affections are
> A sick man's appetite, who desires most that
> Which would increase his evil. He that depends
> Upon your favours, swims with fins of lead,
> And hews down oaks with rushes. (1.1.166–80)[13]

Martius, knowing he is disliked by the plebeians, decides those whom they do favor must be lacking the quality he possesses: greatness. He believes that the only person they will credit is the person who will flatter them, and consequently that person will lose what makes him great. The plebeians are compared to animals who would transform a man into sinking fish and weakened oaks, bereft of human virtue. Martius cannot imagine the plebeians being capable of making political decisions that are rooted in logic—only in appetite. Robin Headlam Wells tells us that a "long tradition of anti-populist satire" depicted the common folk the way the Martius does here.[14] Translated into English from French right before *Coriolanus* was thought to be written was a narrative in which much of Martius's view of the people can be seen:

> The people (we understand here the vulgar sort, the popular rout, a kind of people under what covert soever of base, servile, and mechanical condition) are a strange beast with many heads, and which in few words cannot [but] be described inconstant and variable, without stay, like the waves of the sea: they are moved and appeased, they allow and disallow one and the same thing at one and the same instant; there is nothing more easy than to drive them into what pas-

> sion he will; they love not wars for the true end thereof, nor peace for rest or quietness, but for variety's sake . . . without judgement, reason, discretion. Their judgement and wisdom is but by chance, like a cast at dice, unadvised and headlong of all things, and always ruled by opinion or custom, or the greater number, going all in a line, like sheep that run after those that go before them, and not by reason and truth.[15]

This topical reference hints at a cultural rhetoric in circulation during the sixteenth and early seventeenth centuries that Shakespeare may have heard often, a generalization about the commoners that could be true in some cases, to be sure, as it could in any social group. It is propagandist, and like most propaganda relies on stereotypes and generalizations, neither of which are meant to be logical, just persuasive. Uncovered in Martius's speech, too, is his lack of ability to reflect, as is evident in the populist satire.

This habit of speech that Martius adopts is rhetoric of a supportive nature: Martius draws images that will support his ideas, that will reinforce his beliefs.[16] His inability to reflect,[17] or feel he must reflect, is embedded in his speeches. As Carol Sicherman comments, Martius's language is full of precepts: nineteen of the play's fifty-six precepts[18] are spoken by Martius.[19] Precepts, like clichés, show lack of reflection. Perhaps worse, however, as James Calderwood argues, Martius fails to understand language as a means to communicate feelings, ideas, or even truths beyond the limited scope he assigns to words—"he invests his words with meaning in one sense by being 'constant' to his word, his promise" (214).[20]

First Citizen anticipates the harangue, the "good word," of Martius. In the introduction to the citizens, however, we see little evidence that the people are irrational or animal-like, just frustrated.[21] Martius we see as agitated, arrogant, just as we see him in his final moments. His banishment from Rome only increases his agitation with Rome and its republic—he will come to believe that his banishment affirms what he believes about giving the people a voice, that they can never make any but ill-informed decisions. Part of what he claims to be true of the plebeians is immediately confirmed, when Martius is called to duty against the Volsces. Martius tells the citizens, whom he calls rats, that the Volscians have grain and that they are welcome to fight for it. The stage direction "Citizens steal away. Sicinius and Brutus remain" must affect readers one way or the other regarding their attitude toward the mob. Their "stealing" does suggest that they are the cowards Martius claims, that is, if we agree with Martius that those who do not wish to fight are cowards. For Martius, it can be no other. We can see Rome from the perspective of the plebeians or that of Martius in Shakespeare's play. We are introduced to a Martius who is faithful to his ideals to the point of being uncivil and to a populace who are unwilling to follow Martius to war. Martius inspires no hunger for honor, and the people's hunger for food, not for becoming food for the enemy, is not altogether unreasonable.

Martius finds himself rejected by plebeians who are unmoved by his taunting sarcasm. Who is Martius to the plebeians in this play? He is a servant of the state, no matter that he paints his service in the color of valor and duty. Around the plebeians, he shows his agitation with them. Three times, he becomes so upset with their request for corn that he keeps cursing them with "hang ye" and "hang 'ems." When Menenius tells Martius what the seditious citizens want, Menenius says, "corn at their own rates. They say / The city is well stor'd" (1.1.188–89), to which Martius says, "Hang 'em!" and then mocks Menenius's "they say" by retorting, "They say!" / They'll sit by the fire and presume to know / What's done i'th' Capitol who's like to rise, / Who thrives, and who declines." (1.1.189–92). Martius cannot bear that the citizens would have a voice, an opinion, on matters of government. It is abhorrent to the elitist Martius.

Shakespeare puts the term *opinion* to use in several ways: one meaning is "voice," and the other is "reputation." The tribunes Sicinius and Brutus, Martius's antagonists,[22] entered the first act at Scene One, line 235, immediately following a messenger's telling Martius of the Volscians preparing to fight Rome. Silently, they listen to Martius, Cominius, Titus Lartius, Menenius, and others discuss the battle plan; they have also heard Martius invite the rebelling citizens to follow him to Volscian territory to get corn. The tribunes find him proud, yet they fear the "opinion" that the people might side with him if he is successful in war (1.1.270). Martius cannot brook the opinion of the people on governmental matters, but his entire life depends on opinion: his opinion of what a Roman should be, which in turn is affirmed by his triumphs in battle. His successes are trumpeted in Rome. Because successes are valued, the people's opinion of Martius can remain positive. The tribunes know Martius's opinion of tribunes and representation; thus, it is the opinion of the people toward Martius that the tribunes must control if they are to retain their positions.

The term *opinion* is picked up in Act One, Scene Two, just eight lines later in in the setting of Corioles. The First Senator says to Aufidias, "So, your opinion is, Aufidias, / That they of Rome are enter'd in our counsels, / And know how we proceed" (1–3). First Senator might have said "belief" or another term, but Shakespeare has just used "opinion" in several contexts, and now in another. Aufidias's opinion or belief is that Rome knows the Volscian plans for an attack on Rome, that in fact, as the following passage suggests, Rome is always on guard to Volscian business: "What ever have been thought on in this state / That could be brought to bodily act, ere Rome / Had circumvention?" (1.2.4–6).

"Opinion" indicates judgment: for Martius, his opinion or Aufidias's opinion is invested with authority. Martius derives his authority from his patrician status. For Martius, the "superiority of the patrician class," as Ronald Knowles suggests, is the "unconditional absolute" (1.2.145) at the root of all arguments that he forwards to either plebeian or patrician regarding the plebeians having a voice, an opinion. Martius's elitism was nurtured in him by his mother, Volumnia. Shakespeare draws attention to the term *opinion* by having it uttered by three major players in this tragedy. Aufidias will murder Martius, who is banished by the Romans at the tribunes' manipulation of the people's opinion. Martius's naive faith in the superiority of the patricians leads him to articulate his opinions on the plebeians having a voice in a vituperative manner that earns him the scorn of the Romans. In fact, the Volscians are privy to this fact. In Act One, Scene Two, Aufidias is reading to First Senator a letter that he has received on the Roman plan to strike the Volscians. A phrase from one of the sentences reads: "Martius your old enemy / (Who is of Rome worse hated than you) . . . lead on this preparation" (1.2.12–15). Even outside the walls of Rome, into enemy hands has fallen information that compromises the reputation of Martius and makes him vulnerable, the very condition he believes his elitism and his strength will ward off.[23]

In the following scene, the source of Martius's elitist attitude is introduced to the audience. Act One, Scene Three, opens with Volumnia chiding her daughter-in-law, Virgilia: "I pray you, daughter, sing, or express yourself in a more comfortable sort. If my son were my husband I should freelier rejoice in that absence wherein he won honour" (1–4). Volumnia, unlike Virgilia, is thrilled that Martius is in battle again, for it is in battle that Martius wins glory, and he brings that glory home to his mother, his family name. Volumnia's "sing" and "rejoice" express the euphoria she feels over her son's successes in battle. She explains to listening Virgilia:

> I, considering how honor would become such a person . . . was pleased to let him seek danger where he was like to find fame. To a cruel war I sent him, from whence he returned, his brows bound with oak. (1.3.9–15)

Volumnia, fascinated with the Roman ideal of honor which she herself cannot gain,[24] nurtures her child with images of valor, glory, honor, and military action. She swells with pride imagining her son at that very moment fighting:

> Methinks I see him stamp thus, and call thus:
> "Come on you cowards, you were got in fear
> Though you were born in Rome." His bloody brow
> With his mail'd hand then swiping, forth he goes
> Like to a harvest man that's task'd to mow
> Or all, or lose his hire. (1.3.32–37)

The agricultural metaphor glances at Martius's comment to the plebeians to follow him to battle the Volscians if they want corn. Here, too, we hear Volumnia's stereotype of the common Romans as cowards, which she has apparently passed on to her son. Volumnia thinks little of men who do not thrill at the thought of military valor and its attendant violence. Imitating Martius stamping and name-calling, Volumnia role-plays the soldier she can never become. Virgilia, not sharing Volumnia's love of Roman military aggressiveness, interjects that she does not want her husband bloody or battling Aufidias. Not all Romans feel as Volumnia and her son do, even those from the patrician class. Virgilia's fears are normal responses, and not unfounded. Volumnia, like her son, appeals to abstractions, ideals of warrior-hood, which allow her to imagine her son as transcending mortal norms. Elevating him to such a status allows her also to see him as invincible, just as he sees himself. Neither is reflective.

Understanding Coriolanus's mother is critical to understanding what drives or motivates Martius. Volumnia's fantasy of the great Roman warrior is a fantasy of propagandist literature that Shakespeare, but perhaps not the "real" Volumnia, may have known or learned. Shakespeare's early seventeenth-century Anglo drama on republican Rome is a decidedly early modern English interpretation of a historico-political past circulated by schoolmasters, translators, and chroniclers of England's past.[25] Volumnia is Shakespeare's creation, not Plutarch's, although it is possible that Shakespeare had read Plutarch's *The Sayings of Spartan Women*, observes Coppélia Kahn. Plutarch supplies anecdotes of Roman mothers who seek glory for their state through their sons (146). Roman mothers, it has been argued by E. Cantarella, were respected in ancient Roman culture not only for bearing sons, but also for the role they played in the "transmission of a culture" (qtd. in Kahn 147). Volumnia exemplifies the woman in a social order who perversely upholds or supports an ideology that in praxis is as likely to bring her emotional pain or loss as not. Rather than subvert the patriarchal social order that in truth oppresses not only the nonelite but also women, Volumnia chooses to immerse herself into the culture's warrior-aggressor roots, taking credit for her son's successes. She feeds on images of his violated and bloody flesh, on his killing and destroying. When Valeria, a friend of Volumnia, enters the scene, Valeria tells an anecdote about Virgilia and Martius's son, Martius, that amplifies the Martian family's bloodlust. Valeria exclaims of the young Martian:

> O'my word, the father's son! I'll swear 'tis a very pretty boy. O'my troth, I looked upon him o' Wednesday half an hour together: 'has such a confirmed countenance. I saw him run after a gilded butterfly, and when he caught it, he let it go again, and after it again, and over and over he comes, and up again, catched it again; or whether his fall enraged him, or how 'twas, he did so set his teeth and tear it. Oh, I warrant how he mammocked it! (1.3.57–65)

To which Volumnia replies: "One on's father's moods" (1.3.66). The fragile insect being shredded by the boy is perceived as a manly gesture, a sign that he will grow, like Martius, to use his mood or rage as a reason to destroy. Volumnia could not imagine that fragile creature as analogous to her own son, who will be brutally slain. Ironically, the son will destroy his father, when he appears with his mother and grandmother to plead for Rome later in the play. When Caius Martius looks on his son and family, he cannot help but agree not to destroy Rome, yet he knows that it will cost him his life. Metaphorically, the butterfly is emblematic of the fragility that Martius works hard to escape, to repress; in his ambitious trek to supremacy on the battlefield, Martius can be nearly godlike. Volumnia's boastful claim to Virgilia that Martius will "beat Aufidias's head below his knee / And tread upon his neck" (1.3.46–47) is brutally imaged in Aufidias's stomping on Martius's dead body. While Martius dies, Volumnia is credited with saving Rome from the monster of a son she has created.

Here, early in the play, well before the irony of Volumnia's words strike home, the audience learns that Martius values Roman *virtus*, that he is politically conservative, that he finds the plebeians' having a voice reprehensible and unnecessary, and that his mother might be responsible for his elitist perspective on Roman life. Volumnia's description of her devotion to raising a warrior for the state follows two scenes that have introduced characters important to Coriolanus's tragedy: Menenius, a patrician mentor to Coriolanus, the plebeians, the tribunes, Cominius,

Titus Lartius, and Aufidias. At this point, however, Martius is on the verge of carving out a name for himself, a name that put him in the historical narratives of ancient writers. This moment is delayed in the play by the women chatting among themselves on stage. Valeria, who wants Virgilia and Volumnia to visit a woman who is ready to give birth, attempts to entice the modest and worried Virgilia to leave the house. Virgilia insists on remaining at home, saying that "I'll not over the / threshold till my lord return from the wars" (1.3.74–75). Valeria teases her as she sews, calling her a Penelope awaiting her Ulysses: "yet they say, all the yarn she spun in Ulysses' absence did but fill Ithaca full of moths" (1.3.82–84). The moth, the ruin of fabric, like the suitors who visited Penelope and would undermine the fabric of her family, is an image of destruction. Again, this scene anticipates an unraveling of a unit, that of the Martians. Volumnia is too caught up in her fantasy of Martius to sense the disturbance invoked by Valeria's witty taunt. When Valeria has succeeded in convincing Virgilia to leave the house, by claiming to know something of the battle with the Volsces, Volumnia imperiously states, "Let her alone, lady; as she is now, she will but disease our better mirth" (1.3.103–4). Volumnia likes her mood. Virgilia stays home.

This scene establishes what comprises Martius's family unit, the influence Volumnia has had on Martius's life as a soldier, not to mention her dominance in the household. Virgilia figures mostly as an antithesis to Volumnia, a Martian in name only. We also see a group of people who love and respect Martius; until this point, the audience has seen only people who find him proud and a threat to their livelihood. Thus, when Scene Three transitions into Scene Four, a more sympathetic, if not romanticized, picture of Caius Martius emerges.

The domestic setting of Scene Three transforms into a battleground at Corioles as Martius and Titus Lartius walk on stage to be met by a messenger. Drums and colors accompany them. Martius speaks to Titus first, in a tone of friendly camaraderie. He bets Titus that the Roman general has talked with the enemy; Titus offers that they wager their horses. Martius loses the wager with grace and spirit, as the two armies had yet to meet. Titus, of course, does not cash in. In this exchange, Martius shows us a man comfortable with himself. This is the first we see him as confident and likeable. Among equals, Martius is in control of himself and emotions, which is not true of the Martius we first meet. His bullying of the plebeians shows a personality open to loss of control.

Once it has been established that the generals have not met, Titus wants to "summon the town [Corioles]" (1.4.7), but Martius first wants to know where the Volscian army is. The messenger says a mile and a half. The landscape is thus situated for the audience. In front of the walls of Corioles, Titus and Martius are close enough to the Volscian and Roman armies in the field to hear their "alarum," or call to battle. In a heroic vein Martius petitions,

> Now Mars, I prithee make us quick in work,
> That we with smoking swords may march from hence
> To help our fielded friends. Come, blow thy blast. (1.4.10–12)

Martius's plan is to slay whom he can at Corioles and then take his army to the field to help the Roman army. Ambitious Martius imagines what he can accomplish in a short time over a wide area. The stage for this plan is not before our eyes but in our imaginations, showing us the limitless boundaries of those who free themselves from mortal boundaries and push beyond.

Titus's blast toward Corioles's walls produces *two senators and others*. Martius asks whether Tullus Aufidias is there. A senator responds, "No, nor a man that fears you less than he / That's lesser than a little" (1.4.14–15). This boasting comment is followed by the sound of a drum heard in the distance. The senator says,

> Hark, our drums
> Are bringing forth our youth. We'll break our walls
> Rather than they shall pound us up; our gates
> Which yet seem shut, we have but pinn'd with rushes;
> They'll open of themselves. Hark you, far off!
> *Alarum far off.*
> There is Aufidius. List what work he makes
> Amongst your cloven army.
> Oh, they are at it!

The senator assures Titus and Martius that the Volscians were prepared against the Roman threat. Their gates, which give the appearance of security, only mask the army that will soon rush through. Worse, Aufidias has broken the ranks of the Romans. Martius and Titus see that they are mocked, Martius exclaiming, "they fear us not, but issue forth the city" (1.4.23). In turn, Martius's mood changes at the bold provocation of the Volsces:

> They do disdain us much beyond our thoughts,
> Which makes me sweat with wrath. Come on, my

fellows:
He that retires, I'll take him for a Volsce,
And he shall feel mine edge. (1.4.26–29)

His wrath very quickly is directed at his own soldiers, as the stage directions tell us: *Alarum. The Romans are beat back to their trenches.* Martius, we are told, enters cursing:

All the contagion of the south light on you,
You shames of Rome! You herd of—boils and plagues
Plaster you o'er, that you may be abhorr'd
Farther than seen, and one infect another
Against the wind a mile! You souls of geese,
That bear the shapes of men, how have you run
From slaves that apes would beat! Pluto and hell!
All hurt behind, backs red, and faces pale
With flight and agued fear! Mend and charge home,
Or, by the fires of heaven, I'll leave the foe
And make my wars on you. Look to't. Come on;
If you'll stand fast, we'll beat them to their wives,[26]
As they us to our trenches. Follow me! (1.4.30–42)

Martius's blistering admonishment of his fellow soldiers is shot through with the maledictions and name calling that we have already heard from him in Act One, Scene One. His frustration at the soldiers may be warranted, but his tendency to verbal insult indicates a loss of emotional control. Wrath may put him in the mood to fight the enemy, but here he wastes his agitation on men he needs to lead against the Volscians. Whatever his feelings are about soldiers who run from battle, on the battlefield, every soldier counts as a member of the corps. Martius isolates himself from the others when he curses them.[27] We have already seen him lose an audience when the plebeians steal away from him. Now, he alienates his soldiers. When Martius sees the gates of Corioles open, he sees an opportunity and says, "'Tis for the followers Fortune widens them, / Not for the fliers. Mark me, and do the like!" (1.4.44–45). In other words, Martius sees the opening gates as an opportunity for the Romans and a threat to the Volscians trying to return to their city (fliers). The comment presumes that Fortune is on the side of those who take advantage of opportunities. Only Martius enters the gates, however, as his soldiers prove not of his mettle. "Foolhardiness! not I," (1.4.46) says the First Soldier. "Nor I," says the Second Soldier. All watch as Martius is closed in, which affirms for them they have done the right thing. Thus, Martius's isolation is sealed physically and emotionally.

Titus Lartius enters the scene and asks the soldiers where Martius is, to which the First Soldier responds, "Slain, sir, doubtless" (1.4.48), having "follow[ed] the fliers" (1.4.49). This news leads Titus to express sentiments about Martius that not only elevate Martius's status as superior among soldiers but also prepare us for what will follow:

> Oh noble fellow!
> Who sensibly outdares his senseless sword,
> And when it bows, stand'st up. Thou are left, Martius:
> A carbuncle entire, as big as thou art,
> Were not so rich a jewel. Thou wast a soldier
> Even to Cato's wish, not fierce and terrible
> Only in strokes, but with thy grim looks and
> The thunder-like percussion of thy sounds
> Thou mad'st thine enemies shake, as if the world
> Were feverous and did tremble. (1.4.52–61)

Martius is flesh and blood, "sensible," says Titus, whereas a sword cannot feel or sense. The word *carbuncle*,[28] a red jewel, is fiery like the flesh and blood soldier, whose "looks" cause a fever in the world. Not "fierce and terrible," Martius is singularly a model Roman soldier. In truth, Martius is a Roman, a man raised to be a soldier. He may curse his soldiers and the plebeians, express his frustration in an ugly manner, but we also see him inviting them to join him in battle. Because he has been raised to believe being a soldier is the Roman way, he believes all Romans feel the same way, and in this, he is too severe.

Upon Titus's last word, Martius enters the scene, bleeding, the flesh-and-blood soldier of Titus's encomium realized. Seeing him, Titus and all the soldiers enter the city and assault the Volscians. The fantastic sight of the bloodied Martius, a man left alone to battle the enemy, might have stirred others to fight, invoked thoughts of bravery in the audience. Yet as the men rush into Corioles, the scene closes, and in Scene Five, the abstract glory that is sought by Martius is sullied by the appearance of soldiers griping about the spoils they have taken from Corioles. At the sound of a trumpet, Martius and Titus then reenter the scene. Martius cannot refrain from keeping his thoughts to himself:

> See here these movers, that do prize their hours
> At a crack'd drachma! Cushions, leaden spoons,
> Irons of a doit, doublets that hangmen would

> Bury with those that wore them, these base slaves,
> Ere yet the fight be done, pack up. Down with them! (1.5.4–8)

Martius may be right, that the spoils are worthless, as the soldiers say as much. That he must comment upon it, that he must call soldiers slaves when they do not act as he would, shows contempt for them.[29] Yet, again, as he has in past complaints, Martius presumes they will follow him or Titus into battle. Hearing Cominius's trumpet, in the middle of his tirade, Martius tells Titus to "take convenient numbers to make good the city, / Whilst [he], with those that have the spirit, will haste / To help Cominius" (1.5.12–14). Aufidias is battling Cominius's troops, and Martius wants to fight Aufidias to test his strength. His mind is not on who follows, but on his own quest.

Because Martius bleeds so profusely, Titus tells Martius, "Worthy sir, thou bleed'st; / Thy exercise hath been too violent / For a second course of fight" (1.5.14–16). Martius takes this as a compliment, responding, "Sir praise me not; / My work hath yet not warm'd me" (1.5.16–17). Martius presumes his bloodied body means he has fought well, not that he risks death. He identifies wholly with his pierced flesh; "My soul's hate, Aufidias," says Martius, has been "piercing our Romans" (1.5.10–11). As a pierced Roman, Martius sees the other pierced Romans probably more in the abstract than real. What are real to Martius are Aufidias, fighting him, and winning. His reward will be the glory that he will bring his family name.

Warmed by Martius's amazing strength and will, Titus is moved to ask for divine intervention:

> Now the fair goddess, Fortune,
> Fall deep in love with thee, and her great charms
> Misguide thy opposers' swords! Bold gentleman,
> Prosperity be thy page! (1.5.20–23)

As the lover of a goddess and a person of gentle status, Martius is ennobled by Titus's petition. And so it has gone through Act One, that we have seen multiple sides to Martius: the patricians and upper-rank soldiers find him semi-divine, whereas the plebeians and other Romans find him a tyrant. In the next scene, Six, which follows Martius's exit, Cominius and his soldiers, having retired from their fighting with the Volscians, are met by a messenger who tells them that Titus and Martius have been beaten to the trenches and that he brought Cominius the news as soon as he could. Not knowing the condition of his army at the gates, Cominius is gladdened when he sees Martius enter the scene and hears Martius ask, "Come I too late?" (1.6.24). Cominius, like Titus and Volumnia, sees Martius as superior to other men. He responds,

> The shepherd knows not thunder from a tabor,
> More than I know the sound of Martius' tongue
> From every meaner man. (1.6.25–27)

Shakespeare here uses another character to paint strokes of nobility on Martius and subsequently distinguish him from the meaner or common sort. With Martius's nobility being affirmed by patricians and soldiers, Martius has little doubt of his worth in his culture. When Martius recognizes Cominius, he greets him with warmth and high emotion:

> Oh! let me clip ye
> In arms as sound as when I woo'd; in heart
> As merry as when our nuptial day was done,
> And tapers burn'd to bedward. (1.6.29–32)

Martius giddily looks forward to what is to come on the battlefield as if he were a bridegroom. The exercise of battle excites him. The intimate bonds he feels with men like Titus and Cominius he can liken to a heterosexual relationship. Martius is a man of many passions, yet negative ones seem to dominate. In the exchange of information between Cominius and Martius concerning the taking of Corioles, Martius shows generosity toward the messenger who told Cominius that the Romans had been dominated by the Volscians by telling Cominius not to punish him, but as for the troops that Martius led, he lacks charity. He tells Cominius, "but for our gentlemen, / The common file—a plague! tribunes for them!—" (1.6.42–43). Still at the forefront of Martius's thoughts is the plebeians' gaining representation, so much is he rankled by the right to a voice given to men he feels are so undeserving of a right that he possesses. His expectation of the common soldier is severe and unrealistic. Common soldiers were not trained from a young age to win, to live for winning battles and bringing glory to Rome. Martius, on the other hand, enjoys testing himself on the battlefield, as the next passage suggests.

When Martius discovers that Cominius and his troops have not taken the field, he asks, "set me against Aufidias and his Antiates" (1.6.59). Cominius would rather he rest and clean his wounds, but Martius protests. At this moment in the play, we see Martius as conflict free as we are likely to see him. Warmed by his finding Cominius, by the blood flowing from his wounds, Martius is a soldier, surrounded by soldiers, and his comfort level is high, as indicated by his speech to the soldiers:

> Those are they
> That most are willing. If any such be here—
> As it were sin to doubt—that love this painting
> Wherein you see me smear'd; if any fear
> Lesser his person than an ill report;
> If any think brave death outweighs bad life,
> And that his country's dearer than himself;
> Let him alone, or so many so minded,
> Wave thus to express his disposition,
> And follow Martius. (1.6.66–75)

Martius sounds the theme he knows best: losing blood for the state, for Rome. State and family come before self. His speech hits home, as the soldiers respond: "O me alone! Make you a sword of me!" (1.6.76).[30] This group of soldiers is not like those he has just cursed. In fact, the stage directions note: *They take him up in their arms, and cast up their caps*. The stage directions frequently call for the casting in the air of caps, an action that from start to finish ties the play together. The casting in the air of caps by the soldiers signals their recognition of the deeds accomplished by Martius. But it also signals a consensus by a group of men, as it does so often throughout the play. The first mention of caps being tossed into the air came when Martius was mocking the plebeians being granted the right to representation. He tells Menenius that "they threw their caps / As they would hang them on the horns o'th'moon, / Shouting their emulation" (1.1.211–13).

The height to which the plebeians threw their caps, in Martius's eyes, matched the decibel level of their shouts. Their joy is shown in the consensus of shouts and cap tossing. The soldiers tossing their caps parallels the action of the plebeians, the one act an ordinary expression by soldiers, the other an act loathed by Martius. For Martius, who cannot see any relationship between devoted soldiers and the plebeians, the cap-tossing cues the audience to the diversity of Rome's people, to their common habits, to which Martius is blind. The Roman that Martius recognizes as Roman is narrowly defined: patrician and soldier.

Raised in the air by the soldiers, Martius literally and metaphorically has the support of his soldiers. From this group, he selects the strongest to fight the Volsces, telling the rest that they have duties enough to obey. Martius thanks them, however, showing graciousness that he exhibits to few in the play. When we next see Martius, in Act One, Scene Eight, he meets Aufidias. The setup of the scene is simple: each enters from one of the side stage doors. Martius speaks first to Aufidias, saying, "I'll fight with none but thee, for I do hate thee / Worse than a promise-breaker" (1.8.1–2). The comparison that Martius invokes indicates that he values the spoken word in contracts between people. Their integrity lies in the speech, not just the deed, for Martius. The hatred Martius bears toward people who cannot keep their word becomes significant later in the play, when Martius's seat for consul is challenged by the two-faced tribunes and plebeians.

To fire Aufidias into a fighting rage, Martius tells Aufidias that the blood with which he is smeared is not his own, but the blood of the Volscians: "Alone I fought in your Corioles walls, / And made what work I pleas'd" (1.8.8–9). Martius wants to be tested in battle; having the city to himself was not enough. Now he wants the greatest warrior that he knows to fight him, so that he may win and bring even more glory upon his name. The two fight, but Aufidias's men come to his aid, and the scene ends without Martius achieving his goal of slaying Aufidias.

In Scene Nine, a retreat is sounded, and a bandaged Martius is shown entering the scene, alone, through one stage door, whereas the Roman army enters from the other door, led by Cominius. Martius's separation from the other Roman soldiers and military men is significant. The process of his losing his identity as a Roman solider and a member of the Roman corps has already begun, prominently evident when we hear him brag that he alone took Corioles. But little by little, Martius questions Roman practices, making himself vulnerable to enemies inside and outside Rome.

For instance, Cominius begins the scene by announcing that he will report Martius's great deeds to the senators, patricians, and "fusty plebeians" (1.9.7). Immediately, Titus Lartius enters with his band of men, praising Martius. In response, Martius asks that they say no more, that each soldier who did his job the best that he could was not to be praised less. Cominius says that "Rome must know / The value of her own" (1.9.20–21) and offers Martius one-tenth of all gained that day for his work. Martius refuses, saying, "I do refuse it, / And stand upon my common part with those / That have beheld the doing" (1.9.38–40). The reply wins the hearts of the soldiers, who throw their caps into the air to show their approval, with their lances held high. Cominius then gives Martius the name Coriolanus, which he accepts, again, to the delight of his soldiers. Martius has one request of Cominius, to give succor to an elderly man who hosted Martius in his home and treated him well. Cominius wants to oblige him, but Martius cannot remember the name of the old man. Martius shrugs it off, asking for drink, never mentioning the man again, showing, it seems, the increasing disaffectedness Martius is feelings from others. The last scene of Act One brings Aufidias on stage to tell us his hate for Martius has grown to the point that he wishes to "wash [his] fierce hand in's heart" (1.10.27). Envy, not honor, rules Aufidias, and Martius mistakes in thinking the case could be otherwise. Admiring Aufidias for his martial prowess is as ruinous to Martius as his loathing of a right to representation by the plebeians. Unless all the people with whom Martius communicates his feelings value the ideals of Rome as he does, he makes himself vulnerable.

Act Two opens in Rome with Menenius and the two tribunes, both of whom, like Aufidias, hate Martius. Menenius knows this and, comforted by the knowledge from "the augurer" that Rome may hear good news that evening, presses the tribunes about their hatred of Martius. "Who does the wolf love?" he asks the two old men, who respond, "the lamb" (2.1.6–7). Menenius says, "Ay, to devour him, as the hungry plebeians would the noble Martius" (2.1.8–9). The notion of Martius being a lamb, an emblem or symbol of innocence, among others, seems odd, given Martius's tough exterior. On the other hand, Martius is innocent, or more concisely, naive about politics. Martius is an unusually virtuous man, but his severity in their practice puts others off. The tribunes claim to Menenius that Martius's chief vices are pride and being boastful. Menenius takes the opportunity to tell the tribunes how proud they are, not to mention how little loved they are by the patricians. Menenius, of course, who is a patrician and very fond of Martius, is not likely to look kindly upon the tribunes. "You are ambitious for poor knaves' caps and legs," insists Menenius (2.1.68).[31] The mention of caps at this point is to their being removed, not thrown, but certainly the caps symbolize approval. The tribunes have no position without the plebeians, whom they have been appointed to represent. Doffing their hats, the plebeians recognize the tribunes as bearing power. In contrast, as soon as Menenius leaves the tribunes, he runs into Volumnia, Virgilia, and Valeria, who tell them Martius is soon to arrive. Menenius, excited by the news, shouts, "Take my cap, Jupiter, and I thank thee. Hoo! / Martius coming home?" (2.1.104–105). Menenius doffs his cap to the heavens, to Jupiter, in thanks, not to recognize the undeserving. In no way can the tribunes be seen as efficient and useful in their positions, for as Menenius recounts their failings in the first scene of Act Two, the tribunes do not protest. Instead, they keep saying Menenius behaves as badly as they do.

Martius's entry into the city is announced, his deeds and new name reported. He greets his waiting family in turn, while Menenius welcomes him, telling him there are those who have yet to accept Martius, that is to say, the tribunes. The envious tribunes, taking in the scene of the patricians closing ranks, begin to fret about how Martius will be received. As Martius, Cominius, Menenius, and Martius's family leave the scene, the tribunes reveal their fears that Martius will put them out of office if he gains any political power, which is likely because of his valiant exploits. A messenger arrives to bid them to the senate and confirms what they most fear:

> 'Tis thought
> That Martius shall be consul.
> I have seen the dumb men throng to see him, and
> The blind to hear him speak. Matrons flung gloves,
> Ladies and maids their scarfs and handkerchers,
> Upon him as he pass'd; the nobles bended
> As to Jove's statue, and the commons made
> A shower and thunder with their caps and shouts:
> I never saw the like. (2.1.258–66)

Once again, caps are tossed as a sign of approbation of Martius, this time by the plebeians, a group for whose approval Martius little cares. Thus, as a parallel to the patrician and warrior cap-tossing, the image of the plebeians' shower of caps, the sheer number, is telling to the tribunes, who would rather not a shout or cap were tossed in Martius's honor.

The meeting of senators, Martius, Cominius, Menenius, the patricians, the tribunes, and lictors in the senate opens Scene Two of Act Two. Menenius announces the purpose of the meeting is to honor Martius for his service. The First Senator asks Cominius to begin to describe Martius's deeds, when Sicinius and Brutus interject to let the senate know that they will consider Martius too "if he [would] remember / a kinder value of the people than / He hath hitherto priz'd them at" (2.2.59–60). At this point, they begin to agitate Martius, whom they know to be easily provoked. Although Menenius asks them to keep silent, Martius rises to leave, knowing he cannot keep peace with the tribunes in the room. Menenius asks him to stay, and the First Senator, not knowing why Martius attempts to leave, tells him "never shame to hear / What you have nobly done"

(2.2.67–68) to which Martius responds, "I had rather have my wounds to heal again / Than hear say how I got them" (2.2.69–70). Martius, finding himself in another uncomfortable setting, shows his vulnerability to his short temper in front of the two men who can most easily ruin him. Claiming that he cannot "sit idly" and hear his "nothings monster'd" (2.2.76–77), Martius leaves the room. Cominius, nonetheless, recounts Martius's deeds of courage and service to Rome for the senators and patricians. Martius, we discover, at sixteen first served Rome as a warrior (2.2.87) and had been in seventeen conflicts since (2.2.100). We know his exploits at Corioles.

Cominius's speech wins the confidence of the group, and the First Senator votes to honor Martius. Called to the room, Martius is told by Menenius that he will be consul once he appears before the people in the gown of humility and asks for their approval. Martius asks that he be allowed to "o'erleap that custom," for as he says:

> I cannot
> Put on the gown, stand naked, and entreat them
> For my wounds' sake to give their suffrage. Please you
> That I may pass this doing. (2.2.136–39)

Martius abhors the fact that the plebeians have a voice, a right to representation. That they participate in his election to consul he cannot imagine, despite the fact that it is an old Roman tradition for a candidate for consul to stand before the people in a gown of humility, hatless, and ask for their voices. The most valiant and virtuous servant of Rome is politically opposed to plebeian suffrage. He need only win the voice of the people to become consul, and then, from his position of power, urge a politically conservative approach to representation. The tribunes know this. Menenius knows this. Yet so repugnant is the idea to Martius of standing before the people that he cannot keep his thoughts to himself: "It is a part / That I shall blush in acting" (2.2.144–45); says the indignant Martius,

> To brag unto them, thus I did, and thus,
> Show them th' unaching scars which I should hide,
> As if I had receiv'd them for the hire
> Of their breath only! (2.2.147–50)

Martius references the people's right to a voice, a "breath," as he has from the play's start. He cares not for tradition. His concern is plebeian rights. His healing wounds he feels represent his service to Rome. Service is an abstract ideal. Martius charges that the tradition of showing wounds smacks of the mercantile, as if soldiers gathered them to trade for voices. Yet we know Martius's complaint lacks weight, because his wounds, though perhaps not viewed by the patricians and senators, certainly earned him their vote. Martius would not even be allowed to stand before the people had the senate not approved him. This he ignores.

The plebeians are more charitable toward Martius than he is toward them. Of the seven or eight citizens who open Scene Three, three citizens speak, discussing the power that they have to vote for or against Martius. Third Citizen says,

> We have power in ourselves to do it, but it is a power that we have no power to do. For, if he show us his wounds and tell us his deeds, we are to put our tongue into those wounds and speak for them. So if he tells us his noble deeds, we must also tell him our noble acceptance of them. Ingratitude is monstrous, and for the multitude to be ingrateful, were to make a monster of the multitude of the which we being members, should bring ourselves to be monstrous members. (2.3.4–13)

Third Citizen shows that he recognizes the responsibilities inherent in rights or voice in a corpus or voting body, a talent of which Martius would never admit the plebeians capable. Moreover, the citizen recognizes the monstrosity of abusing the power. "Monstrous members" are threatening because they lack proportion or balance. What Martius fears is a body monstered in size, that is, the plebeians gaining a disproportionate power. The plebeians indicate that they do not wish to be regarded as such, that they wish to show goodwill. The use of synecdoche in putting "tongues into those wounds," in which tongue means voice, draws attention to the voting body as a member of a larger body, the Romans, of which Martius is a member. Martius only wants to be a member of his fantasized, immortalized Rome, perhaps even singled out as special. Zvi Jagendorf points out, as an "aristocrat whose motto is 'Alone,' and who will neither share corn nor power with the people, he is embarrassed by his wounds because, paradoxically, they mark his dependence on the people" (465). That may explain why he never shows them when he puts himself on display in his gown of humility before the people, a critical error on his part. "What must I say?—" (2.3.51) complains Martius to Menenius. In a mocking voice, he practices, "I pray, sir,—Plague upon't! I cannot bring my tongue to such a pace" (2.3.52–53). Whereas the citizens have decided to give Martius's wounds their tongues, he cannot give his tongue, his petition, his speech, to them. The reciprocal relationship between politicians and their constituents requires tact and charity, which is displayed by the citizens, but not Martius.

The citizens show that they believe in a form of government in which those in power should deserve their positions, not to mention work toward social good. Martius believes in a form of government in which only those from the better social ranks should rule. The lower ranks should accept the decisions made by the ruling order as being in the best interest of each group, no questions asked. Martius's political views are elitist, deeply embedded in his consciousness, or else we would not have seen him recall the rights given to the plebeians at times when his life was most threatened, such as during the battle at Corioles. He is a hero, a celebrated warrior, yet he barks at plebeians and complains about their rights. He perceives the plebeians as lacking what he values: Roman *virtus*. When Menenius asks him to consider how he will be perceived by the people if he is rude to them, he responds, "Hang 'em! / I would they would forget me, like the virtues / Which our divines lose by 'em" (2.3.58–60).

What drives Martius to such undignified behavior is his rigid belief in an ideal of *virtus*, that "lauded the spirit of self-sacrificing patriotism," says Charles Wells, who goes on to say that "[t]o live and die for his country was held to be the highest ambition of its citizens" (95). As an aristocrat, Martius owes the state not only military service, but also civil service,[32] a task he is too intemperate and impolitic to manage. When Menenius tells him to have patience while he stands in his gown of humility, Martius suggests that the plebeians who come before him "wash their faces, / And keep their teeth clean" (2.3.62–63). Here is a man who frequently is washed in the blood, flesh, and bone of the enemy in battle, wasting his breath on the washing habits of the poor. He owes them his time, if he truly wants to fulfill his contract of service to the state. Yet here we find Martius selective about his service to Rome; in truth, he values some ideals, but not all. He does not value his civic responsibility to the people, because it does not bring glory to his family as does his military service.

Martius serves the term of his stand, winning the voice of the plebeians. He was rude to them and managed to send them off without their having seen his wounds. His sardonic and witty repertoire was insulting, but it was overlooked by the charitable plebeians. When the second group of citizens approaches Martius, Fourth Citizen says, "You have deserved nobly of your country, and you have not deserved nobly" (2.3.87–88). Asked to explain, the citizen replies,

> You have been a scourge to her enemies, you have been a rod to her friends; you have not indeed loved the common people. (2.3.90–92)

Martius smartly responds,

> You should account me the more virtuous, that I have not been common in my love. I will, sir, flatter my sworn brother the people, to earn a dearer estimation of them; 'tis a condition they account gentle; and since the wisdom of their choice is rather to have my hat than my heart, I will practise the insinuating nod, and be off to them most counterfeitly; that is, sir, I will counterfeit the bewitchment of some popular man, and give it bountiful to the desirers. Therefore, beseech you, I will be consul. (2.3.93–102)

Martius's aristocratic arrogance is rude enough, but the suggestion that he is virtuous in that he has not been common in his love, that is to say, has "loved" without discrimination, references unchaste behavior. To be chaste hardly implies one is more virtuous, just chaste. Then to suggest that the people are so superficial as to value shows of respect toward them from the aristocracy rather than forthright honesty is simply a rationale for Martius's poor attitude toward the people. He presumes himself superior in his honest and open attitude. He cannot remove his hat for the people without telling them that such an act is false. Caps and hats in this play have meant approval, which Martius cannot bring himself to extend. Worse, he announces to the citizens that he will make much of their voices, but he will not show his scars. His stature as a worthy servant of the state probably awes the citizens to the point that they leave without asking to see the scars or even pressing him to show them. They all give their voices, however.

Martius, alone for a moment, complains that "Better it is to die, better to starve, / Than crave the hire which first we do deserve" (2.3.112–13). So little is required of him, yet he finds the task so repugnant that he would rather be dead? His alienation from his Roman heritage grows, preparing him for later events, later decisions that lead to his banishment.[33] Once his stand has ended, he goes to the senate to accept his new responsibility. In the meantime, the tribunes are able to quiz the citizens and elicit from them the information that Martius did not show his wounds, a requirement of acceptance by the people (2.3.161). Third Citizen notes that Martius was mocking the citizens as he asked for their voices, claiming that Martius was "waving [his hat] in scorn" (2.3.165). This is interesting. Martius has told the second group of citizens that to solicit their voices, he will feign removing his hat in respect. But Third Citizen, a member of the first party of citizens to visit Martius, claims he used his hat to show disdain. Hats are visual cues to the emotions of the hats' owners, as we have seen. Shakespeare exploits the hat as a stage prop. It allows for physicality and movement, and in this case, it is used to keep tensions high. When Sicinius the tribune hears the citizens' report on being mocked, he says, "Why either were you ignorant to see't, / Or, seeing it, of such childish friendliness / To yield your voices?" (2.3.172–74).

Martius may have an issue with the citizens having representation and may behave badly around the citizens. We see here, however, that the tribunes who represent them are worse toward the citizens by comparison. The tribunes exploit the citizens for personal gain, and when the citizens fail them, they insult them. The citizens to this point have not shown themselves to be ignorant or childish, but in the way that Martius's core group of supporting patricians paints him in noble shades, the tribunes paint the citizens in shades of silliness. Brutus, the other tribune, jumps in to say, "Could you not have told him / As you were lesson'd:" (2.3.174–75). The tribunes have coached the citizens, and are disappointed that the citizens, awed by Martius, give him their voices. The citizens, who have made it clear to Martius that he must give them something in return for their voices (2.3.72–73), sound as if they could develop a relationship with Martius. The tribunes, however, want more. If the citizens do not need them, they have no jobs.

To ensure their positions of power, the tribunes want to make sure that Martius is not consul, a position that would allow him to encourage other consuls to relieve the tribunes of their duties. Sicinius and Brutus deliver a blistering admonishment to the citizens, not giving them a chance to speak, for thirty-four lines, saying Martius "was a petty servant to the state, / He was your enemy, ever spake against / Your liberties" (2.3.176–78) or "putting him to rage, / You should have ta'en th'advantage of his choler, / And pass'd him unelected" (2.3.195–97). Clearly, they are using the citizens for their own ends, but the citizens are moved to vote against Martius; they suffer from the same vice as does Martius: pride. They do not like hearing that they have been mocked or that they are gullible. Third Citizen, who all along has suspected Martius, offers that "He's not confirm'd: we may deny him yet" (2.3.207). Third Citizen utilized his power to voice a political opinion, and at that moment, the political future of Martius is lost. Martius cannot brook a plebeian voice; for two acts, he has complained about the plebeian right to a voice, and we know how he is likely to respond. So do the tribunes, who exploit Martius's lack of emotional control.

The people, feeling that they were treated with disdain, agree to find hundreds of plebeians who will speak against Martius at the senate. Had the tribunes not stirred the people into hostility toward Martius, perhaps he would have been named consul. In this play, clearly, the tribunes, not necessarily the people, have been at odds with Martius. They are presented in the play as the antagonists, as disturbers of the peace and order, not the noisy and arrogant Martius, who would have only one voice in the senate, youthful and not all that powerful. It is not so clear that Martius truly hates the people, as the tribunes argue; what he hates is that Roman tradition allows people who have not shown equal valor on the battlefield to make decisions about policy.

In Act Three, Scene One, a Martius innocent of the plot by the tribunes to undo him asks Titus Lartius what he knows about Aufidias and hears that he has alienated himself from Corioles and has moved to Antium (3.1.10–11). Martius no sooner says that he wishes he had cause to fight him (3.1.20) than the two tribunes block his way to the marketplace, although he is with Cominius, Menenius, patricians, and senators. The tribunes suggest that trouble will begin if Martius is seen by the people. Martius, incensed, asks the tribunes:

> Are these your herd?
> Must these have voices, that can yield them now
> And straight disclaim their tongues? What are your offices?
> You being their mouths, why rule you not their teeth?
> Have you not set them on? (3.1.32–36)

Martius has guessed immediately the cause of the potential broil between him and the plebeians, and instead of addressing the immediate problem, begins to rail on the wisdom of giving the people a voice. He claims that is a plot by the tribunes "To curb the will of the nobility: / Suffer't, and live with such as cannot rule, / Nor ever will be rul'd" (3.1.38–40). Martius errs in his thinking: because one privilege has been extended hardly means another right will be given the people, even if it were for the social good. Martius simply does not want to share aristocratic prerogatives with plebeians.

Even Cominius recognizes that the "people are abus'd; set on" (3.1.57). And to be fair to Martius, if the people are easily aroused to speaking against a valiant servant of Rome by two aging tribunes, then perhaps their having a voice does pose a threat, as long as they must accept being represented by tribunes. Martius's temper flares more, leading him to hotly argue:

> For the mutable rank-scented meinie, let them
> Regard me as I do not flatter, and
> Therein behold ourselves. I say again,
> In soothing them, we nourish 'gainst our senate
> The cockle of rebellion, insolence, sedition,
> Which we ourselves have plough'd for, sow'd and scatter'd,
> By mingling them with us, the honour'd number
> Who lack not virtue, no, nor power, but that
> Which they have given to beggars. (3.1.65–73)

Martius's elistist stance lacks any self-consciousness, leading us to believe that he truly believes that a significant difference between classes of people in a community exists, that some are deserving and others are not. Those in positions of power in Martius's vision of Rome earn the position through military service and class. The tribunes' plot to undermine Martius's consulship suggests that perhaps Martius should fear a Rome in which state servants like the tribunes are allowed too much political power. All those who have read this play as one in which Shakespeare supported Martius's position against the rabble have not considered fully what role the tribunes, not the plebeians, play in Martius's tragedy. In response to Martius's complaints about mingling of the social orders, Brutus retorts, "You speak o'th'people / As if you were a god to punish, not / A man of their infirmity" (3.1.79–81). Brutus's words are fighting words. Martius has challenged the right of the people to representation, but he has not said anything that suggests he means to punish. To be sure, Martius does not see himself as a plebeian; but attacking him on the basis of an untruth that he wants to punish, Brutus reveals himself as a dirty fighter. Martius, on the other hand, is honest and open about his feelings, which he probably thinks is virtuous. In contrast to Martius, Brutus and Sicinius only purport to anger Martius, who fails to see what easy prey he is. Sicinius refers to Martius's mind as a poison that "shall" not have an opportunity to poison any further (3.1.85–87).

Martius takes particular offense at Sicinius's use of "shall." While it is not entirely clear why Martius takes offense, whether it is his thinking that Sicinius "uses a form of speech to which he has no right" or it is a term specific to the Roman constitution, it sets him on another tirade which he directs to the "unwise patricians" and "reckless senators" (3.1.90–91). "Shall!"

he begins (3.1.89). For thirty-two lines, Martius explains why the senators have erred in creating a condition in Rome that allowed a man "such as [Sicinius], who puts his 'shall', / His popular 'shall', against a graver bench / Than ever frown'd in Greece" (3.1.104–106). Martius clearly thinks that the Roman system of government with its senate (the graver bench) was superior to that of Greece before Rome allowed the tribunes to be magistrates to the people. As he attempts to continue his argument, his friends try to move him to the marketplace. His point is that there must be one "supreme" (3.1.109) authority or "confusion" (3.1.109) will result. For Shakespeare, confusion would have meant chaos, which we can relate to anarchy. Martius cites Greece and its generous distribution of corn to "people who had more absolute power" (3.1.115) as the "ruin of the state" (3.1.117).

Martius's conservative views are not unlike the views of other patricians and senators, but Rome during Martius's time had reached a point at which it had to explore other forms of government. Rome would fail, eventually, for it would be many centuries before groups of people could manage forms of rule similar to our republic, with a right to vote for state and federal leaders and representatives granted to every adult citizen. Rome is young, still an aggressive warrior state, vulnerable to attack. The plebeians' receiving corn gratis irritates Martius because he believes that if they want corn, they must fight for it. Martius has seen too many plebeians shirk their battlefield duties, and in turn believes they are undeserving cowards. Whether or not this is true, we find Martius arguing the same point that he argued at the play's beginning. The focus returns to corn, food, hunger, the belly, and the body politic. The analogy of the human body to the state, the belly to the senate, is recalled when Martius asks the senators and patricians, "How shall this bosom multiplied digest / The senate's courtesy?" (3.1.130–31), that is, how will the plebeians view the senate's giving them free corn? The gratis corn, undeserved in Martius's eyes, takes on a meaning larger than that of providing nourishment. The distribution of corn provides an opportunity for leveling classes in the Roman state, or so Martius fears. As a patrician, Martius has never had to worry about starving, so he cannot see the corn as being relief for hunger. Instead he feels the decision by the senate to hand out corn has led to a condition that will allow the people to manipulate the senate. Martius finally moves to end his argument to the senators by claiming

> where gentry, title, wisdom,
> Cannot conclude but by the yea and no
> Of general ignorance, it must omit

Real necessities, and give way the while
To unstable slightness. (3.1.143–47)

In essence, Martius asks whether or not he, of aristocratic status and military experience, must be subject to the voice of the people whom he believes cannot make sound decisions. When they gave him their voice, he presumed the rightness of their decision, but now that he has heard that the plebeians do not support his consulship, he must appeal to tradition. And although this speech is made to the senators, it is Sicinius who calls him "a traitor," who "shall answer / As traitors do" (3.1.161–62). Martius responds with,

Thou wretch, despite o'erwhelm thee!
What should the people do with these bald tribunes?
On whom depending, their obedience fails
To th'greater bench. In a rebellion,
When what's not meet, but what must be, was law,
Then were they chosen. In a better hour,
Let what is meet be said it must be meet,
And throw their power i'th'dust. (3.1.162–69)

Martius makes it clear that the tribunes, not the people, are the source of his complaint. He claims that the people obey the tribunes before they obey the law, which he finds wrong. It is the tribunes' power over the people that Martius wishes to control. Brutus next calls this treason, and he calls for the aediles to gather the plebeians and to arrest Martius on charges of treason. When the plebeians arrive, Sicinius is quick to point out that Martius "would take from you all your power" (3.1.180). It is the tribunes' power with which Martius has just argued against, but because the tribunes are in a hurry to incite anger in the people, they misrepresent Martius to the plebeians. What follows is a near riot. First, Sicinius "speaks" for the people when he orders an aedile to

Go call the people; *[Exit Aedile.]*
in whose name myself
Attach thee as a traitorous innovator
A foe to th'public weal. Obey I charge thee,
And follow to thine answer. (3.1.172–74)

He has also ordered an aedile to apprehend Martius. To this point, Martius has made statements regarding his political point of view and questions the way the tribunes abuse the law. Sicinius suggests that this abuse of power be discussed later. Though Martius is loud and tactless, he is only one voice of many. Little suggests that he will with his one voice be able to sway the mature, experienced members of the senate to change their way of government, as the members present have largely tried to quiet him. The tribunes take advantage of the moment, however, to make their move. Just as Martius claims the tribunes do, they flout the law when they abuse their power. Sicinius's speaking for the people in charging a celebrated soldier a traitor is an abuse of power and the law. Sicinius knows that those are fighting words to Martius's ears and that confusion or disorder is likely to occur once the people arrive. The law of any land is meant to keep order, and any action whose purpose is to disorder a people is either unlawful or a perversion of power.

At this point in the play, Shakespeare shows how political power abused causes social chaos. Because the tribunes abuse power, it appears that Shakespeare is showing how giving people representation is likely to result in chaos, but that is not entirely the case. Anyone can abuse a position of power, aristocrat or commoner. The tribunes are convinced that Martius will abuse his power as consul, that he will encourage the other senators to "throw their power in the dust," yet from what we have seen of Martius, we know that though he rails, he will follow the laws of Rome. His naive belief in his rightness and Roman superiority in law and senate is what allows him to be caught off guard by the tribunes.

From the way the tribunes ignite the fury of Martius and the emotions of the plebeians, we can infer that what we are viewing is a form of government that is unstable and that is undergoing a test. When Menenius, for instance, pleads "on both sides more respect" (3.1.179), we see a patrician willing to negotiate both patrician and plebeian needs, not a patrician crying treason or insulting the plebeians. Sicinius, who apparently has attempted to hold Coriolanus for arrest, is told by Cominius, "Aged sir, hands off," followed by Martius's rude "Hence rotten thing! or I shall shake thy bones / Out of thy garments" (3.1.177–78). Menenius's call for respect is answered by Sicinius's telling the newly arrived plebeians, "Here's he that would take from you all your power" (3.1.180). Sicinius as much as admits here that he is the people's power, for it is only the tribunes whom Martius threatens. Brutus then orders the aediles to seize Martius. What follows is shouting and fighting between all groups. "Confusion's near" (3.1.188), claims Menenius, who tries to calm Martius and get the tribunes to calm the people. When Sicinius has the people's attention, he further incites them by saying,

> You are at point to lose your liberties:
> Martius would have all from you, Martius
> Whom late you have nam'd for consul. (3.1.192–94)

Menenius, who expected Sicinius to stop the mob action, shouts, "Fie, fie, fie! / This is the way to kindle, not to quench" (3.1.194–95), which, of course, is the tribunes' purpose, although the nobles are slow to perceive their plot. A senator follows up by pointing out that Sicinius's actions are also a way "To unbuild the city, and to lay all flat" (3.1.196). Both men see Sicinius's actions as those that will lead to riot, yet Sicinius cares not, saying, "what is the city but the people?" and the plebeians pick up the theme, crying, "True, the people are the city" (3.1.197–98). Sicinius's hot response actually does not make much sense; in essence, if the city is unbuilt and laid flat, and the people are the city, then are they not threatened by Sicinius's inciting mob action? Of course they are. In fact, who is more vulnerable in any governmental system than the poor, the lower classes? The tribunes are not concerned about the citizens, as has become obvious; they care about their status, which is manifested in the following line by Brutus: "By the consent of all we were establish'd / The people's magistrates" (3.1.199–200). The people affirm this, as does Menenius, yet the soldier Cominius cannot, for he has seen too much. Of the affirmation, Cominius charges of the tribunes's power to incite the plebeians:

> That is the way to lay the city flat,
> To bring the roof to the foundation,
> And bury all which yet distinctly ranges
> In heaps and piles of ruin. (3.1.202–05)

Cominius recognizes the tribunate as being a valid threat to the city, literally and metaphorically. It appears he has not come to terms with the people's sharing rights with the patricians, and what he now witnesses is proof enough to him that a danger rests in empowering the tribunes. Sicinius, who has not been pacified by Menenius or the people, then says that Martius deserves death, as if Cominius's charge poses a threat to him. Brutus agrees that Martius deserves death, and without considering any legal recourse or Roman law, Sicinius follows with the order to the aediles to "lay hold of him. / Bear him to th'rock Tarpeian, and from thence / Into destruction cast him" (3.1.210–12).[34]

Shakespeare shows how quickly all comes to confusion in Act Three, Scene One. The events that lead to Martius's nearly being slain by the people he has protected from the enemy are staged in such as way as to shock and disturb our sensibilities. Martius has recently marched through the gates of Rome in triumph, with the plebeians cheering him. Now they shout for Martius to "Yield" to the aediles. Martius has not changed from the play's start; he has remained constant, if stubborn, in his ways—but the plebeians have not. Instead, they follow their tribunes as ordered and bring hundreds to speak against Martius's consulship. To agree that Martius should die simply because their tribunes wish it so makes them appear mindless and incapable of making informed decisions, as Martius believes of them already. Martius, in fact, has said nothing for the space of about thirty lines; the stage has been given over to the tribunes, who now have an opportunity to answer Martius's choleric opinions on tribunes. They want blood. They will not have it, however. Menenius manages to gain the attention of the tribunes, with the aid of the aediles, and asks if the tribunes would reconsider what they would "violently redress" (3.1.218). The intemperate Brutus claims, "those cold ways, / That seem like prudent helps, are very poisonous / Where the disease is violent" (3.1.218–20). He is wrong. The ways of the law are not cold, but just. Brutus knows this, but in a hurry to be rid of Martius, he asks the aediles to "Lay hands upon him, / And bear him to the rock" (3.1.220–21).

Finally, we hear from the silent Martius. He draws his sword and says, "No, I'll die here" (3.1.221). Having seen Martius fight the enemy, even alone, we know that Martius is not going to be taken without a fight. He, the patricians, and senators manage to fight off the tribunes and people, with Martius being told to go home until the mob has quieted. In the exchange between the patricians and senators, though, we hear their thoughts on the people and the tribunes, and what they say reveals much about the underlying differences between patrician and plebeian: one group believes the worst about the other.

The patricians and senators, who said little during Martius's tirade against the plebeians, become more vocal as they petition Martius to return home; as one senator puts it, "Leave us to cure this cause" (3.1.233). Brutus has called Martius a "disease," invoking the analogy of the body politic that has become a fixture in the play. The senator referring to the patricians needing to "cure" the cause reminds us of Brutus's mention of a disease, although Menenius's following admonition to Martius "For 'tis a sore upon us / You cannot tent yourself: be gone, beseech you" (3.1.233–34) indicates that a cure is needed for a sore, a disease being much harder to treat. The indignant Martius replies that he wishes the plebeians were barbarians, rather than Romans, implying that he could treat them as murderously as he treats the enemy. As Romans, however, they are still part of Martius's landscape. Impatient, Menenius orders Martius to "Be gone! / Put not your worthy rage into your tongue. / One time will owe another" (3.1.237–39). Martius wishes then to put his rage elsewhere, and boasts that he can take forty men; Menenius claims that he would like to take the two tribunes, but Cominius reminds them that the odds are against them. "Manhood is call'd foolery when it stands / Against a falling fabric" (3.1.244–45); that is, the structure in which these two groups of people are used to operating is unstable in times of high emotion. The mob no longer see the patricians and senators as government authorities: they see them as the enemy. Martius finally leaves with Cominius, with Menenius staying behind to "patch" the breach "With cloth of any colour" (3.1.251). Menenius's hope to "patch" the "falling fabric" in "any colour" is much to hope for, and even if he mends the breach, it is only a temporary fix. The heart of this social order's instability rests in the arrogance of the aristocracy and the people's wishes to participate more fully in political affairs that affect their daily lives. Menenius's thinking that he can patch a falling fabric in any color is a show of arrogance on his part. As he has from the play's start, Menenius has tried to appease a disgruntled Roman citizenry in the most patronizing of ways. He talks to the tribunes and citizens from a position of authority, presuming his superiority in all matters. The organic metaphor of the human body as analogous to political order to which he appealed in Act One, ironically, will be co-opted by the citizens and used against Martius.

Tudor and Stuart English rulers exploited the idea of a political order based on the organic body, with the head being the king and the remaining members serving their functions, for the purpose of coercing political and civil obedience among the citizenry. By the time *Coriolanus* was written, however, the metaphor had been losing its hold on an ever-changing political body, a body whose other members are capable of exploiting the rhetoric of the analogy. We see this in Act Three.[35]

Once Cominius and Martius exit, a patrician tells Menenius that Martius's political future has been jeopardized; Menenius defends Martius, claiming he is too "noble for the world" (3.1.254); that is, he never flatters, a presumed necessity for politic engagement. While they speak, they hear a noise, and the patrician says, "I would they were abed!" (3.1.60). Menenius's wishes are darker: "I would they were in Tiber!" (3.1.261). He knows how difficult it will be to discourage the lynching of Martius. Sicinius asks Menenius for Martius, as he wants to be rid of him quickly; the tribunes reason that if they do not kill Martius, he will kill them. First

Citizen steps forward and says Martius "shall well know / The noble tribunes are the people's mouths / And he their hands" (3.1.268–70). This angry body has refigured the body politic as mouth and hands, words and deeds. The head is not important, the voice is. Who owns the voice, owns the power. Menenius says that Martius has done too much for Rome to deserve death. A member of the body politic, Martius should not be eaten by the body that nourished him (3.1.291). Sicinius responds that Martius is a "disease that must be cut away" (3.1.292). Sicinius has learned how to use the organic body analogy for his own ends. Brutus calls Martius an "infection" who should not be allowed to "spread further" (3.1.306–47). Despite their claims, however, Sicinius and Brutus allow Martius another chance.

Act Three, Scene Two begins with Martius asserting to the nobles that he does not care what the tribunes and people threaten; he will speak the truth. Volumnia, Martius's mother, enters,[36] and Martius asks why she does not support his speaking his mind about the plebeians, as she raised him to regard them with contempt (3.2.7–16).

His mother does not deny what she has taught him. Instead, she admits to him, "I would have had you put your power well on / Before you had worn it out" (3.2.17–18). "Let go," that is, "I don't want to hear this," responds Martius. He is not familiar with the lesson he is getting from his mother on policy. Volumnia chides him for allowing the people to see his disposition "ere they lack'd power to cross you" (3.2.23). Volumnia, like Menenius, wants to see Martius settled as consul, probably for the advantages his position would afford them, but both are still schooling Martius, which suggests they do not know him as any but a person about whom they can boast. Volumnia and Menenius still believe that Martius has a chance at consul, and they would like to see him be rewarded with the seat. A First Senator seems to doubt Martius can win the people, but neither Volumnia nor Menenius hears. Martius asks his mother what he should do, and Menenius suggests that he "return to th' tribunes" and "repent" (3.2.36–37). Martius admits he would not apologize to the gods, much less to the plebeians. This moves Volumnia to tell Martius that he is "too absolute" (3.2.39). She tells him that she has heard him say that "honour and policy" work together in war; what difference is there in peace that prevents Martius from participating in policy? "If it be honour in your wars to seem / The same you are not, which, for your best ends / You adopt your policy, how is it less or worse / That [policy] shall hold companionship in peace / With honour, as in war" (3.2.46–50).

Martius asks why his mother "forces" the argument. His mother has not seen him in war, and, in truth, she does not seem aware that the Martius we see in war is the man he is: he does not dissemble. Volumnia has her son's attention and pursues her argument, telling her son that around the people, it is acceptable and even honorable to dissemble, "in words that are but roted in / Your tongue, though but bastards and syllables / Of no allowance to your bosom's truth" (3.2.55–57). She goes so far as to show her son how to "fawn" to the "general louts" (3.2.66–67).

> I prithee now, my son,
> Go to them, with this bonnet in thy hand,
> And thus far having stretch'd it—here be with them—
> Thy knee bussing the stones—for in such business
> Action is eloquence, and the eyes of th'ignorant
> More learned than the ears—waving thy head,
> Which often, thus, correcting thy stout heart,
> Now humble as the ripest mulberry
> That will not hold the handling; or say to them,
> Thou art their soldier, and being bred in broils,
> Hast not the soft way which, thou dost confess,
> Were fit for thee to use, as they to claim,
> In asking their good loves; but thou wilt frame
> Thyself, forsooth, hereafter theirs, so far
> As thou hast power and person. (3.2.72–86)

Volumnia, of course, goes through the motions that Martius must if he is to win the plebeians. Twice now, we have seen Volumnia play her son's part, imagining him gaining what she fantasizes for herself. Again, as a woman, she cannot participate in earning for herself glory and honor—her son must mediate for her. Martius, an obedient son, agrees to speak to the crowd, especially after Cominius enters to announce that in the city "All's in anger" (3.2.95). Although agreeable, Martius tells them that "You have put me now to such a part which never / I shall discharge to th'life" (3.2.105–106). In other words, he will dissemble, as his mother has suggested.

Martius is not a dissembler, however, and to consider being one brings to mind for him thoughts of emasculation: he'll speak in the voice of a "eunuch" and peer through "schoolboy's tears" (3.2.114, 114–16). Volumnia chides her son again, saying, "At thy choice then: / To beg of thee it is my more dishonour / Than you of them" (3.2.123–25). To appease her, Martius tells his mother he will go to the marketplace as asked. By now, the source of Martius's pride and arrogance is no longer a mystery. He learned it from a mother who wants more from her child than he can give her.[37]

Volumnia does not know her child as well as she thinks, and particularly not as well as the tribunes, who are ready for Martius when he arrives at the marketplace in Act Three, Scene Three. Brutus tells Sicinius as they walk on the stage,

> In this point charge him home, that he affects
> Tyrannical power. If he evade us there,
> Enforce him with his envy to the people,
> And that the spoil got on the Antiates
> Was ne'er distributed. (3.3.1–5)

Neither charge can be substantiated, but either will anger Martius, who is proud of being virtuous and law-abiding. These two, of course, are tyrannical in their plotting. They tell the aediles what the people should do when the tribunes call for "death," "fine," or "banishment," claiming that a right exists in an "old prerogative / And power i'th'truth o'th'cause" (3.3.17–18) for the people to execute when threatened by tyranny.[38] The tribunes also order that once a decision has been made, that the people "not cease, but with a din confused / Enforce the present execution of what [they] chance to sentence" (3.3.20–22). The tribunes need disorder and confusion for their plan to work, and again, Shakespeare is foregrounding the tribunes' power to cause chaos. They have a dupe in Martius, which makes their work easy. "Being once chaf'd, he cannot / Be rein'd again to temperance; then he speaks / What's in his heart, and that is there which looks / With us to break his neck" (3.3.27–30).

Martius's voicing his opinion about governmental matters is not a cause for his neck to be broken, as the tribunes claim. They, not a Roman's heart, disturb the quiet of the city. In contrast, Martius enters the scene, and he petitions that

> Th'honour'd gods
> Keep Rome in safety, and the chairs of justice
> Supplied with worthy men, plant love among's,
> Throng our large temples with the shows of peace
> And not our streets with war. (3.3.33–37)

His blessing is short-lived, as the tribunes, meeting with Martius, take little time in telling him that he is being charged with being a traitor to Rome. First, when Martius asks Sicinius why, being given consent by the people to be consul, he has it denied him, Sicinius will not answer. Instead he raises the people's charges against Martius:

> We charge you, that you have contriv'd to take
> From Rome all season'd office, and to wind
> Yourself into a power tyrannical;
> For which you are a traitor to the people. (3.3.63–66)

The word *traitor* infuriates Martius, who forgets his promise to his mother and Menenius, and begins to curse the people:

> The fires i'th'lowest hell fold in the people!
> Call me their traitor! Thou injurious tribune!
> Within thine eyes sat twenty thousand deaths,
> In thy hands clutch'd as many millions, in
> Thy lying tongue both numbers, I would say
> 'Thou liest' unto thee, with a voice as free
> As I do pray the gods. (3.3.68–74)

Sicinius adds Martius's cursing to the growing list of injuries to the people. And while the people call for death, Sicinius calls for banishment, knowing full well that having Martius thrown off the Tarpeian rock is too risky for Sicinius politically. Menenius reminds Martius of his promise to his mother to plead forgiveness of the tribunes, and despite what all around him are saying, Martius hears only Menenius, and as if he were arguing with his mother, who has asked him to act against his nature, he says,

> Let them pronounce the steep Tarpeian death,
> Vagabond exile, flaying, pent to linger
> But with a grain a day, I would not buy
> Their mercy at the price of one fair word,
> Nor check my courage for what they can give,
> To have't with saying, 'Good morrow.' (3.3.88–93)

The depth of Martius's struggle with his mother's request manifests itself in his emotional reply. He cannot be what she asks, preferring to suffer or die. He cannot humble himself to tribunes who have, in essence, overstated their case against him. As Alexander Leggat points out, Martius is being true to himself, while at the same time revealing much about the state of Rome: "The normal state of Roman politics is war" (200). For Martius to beg the voices of the people is a "charade" (200).

> It is a lie about himself; it is also a lie about the state. It presupposes a cooperative society in which the classes understand each other, recognize each other's interests, and are prepared to bargain. At the same time, by codifying the bargaining process in such a theatrical way, it implicitly admits that the process is not natural. What is natural is class war. (200)

From what we have witnessed thus far to what Sicinius finally charges against Martius, we see an interpretation of Martius through the eyes of power-hungry men:

> For that he has
> As much as in him lies, from time to time
> Envied against the people, seeking means
> To pluck away their power, as now at last
> Given hostile strokes, and that not in the presence
> Of dreaded justice, but on the ministers
> That doth distribute it—in the name o'th'people
> And in the power of us the tribunes, we
> Ev'n from this instant, banish him our city,
> In peril of precipitation
> From off the rock Tarpeian, never more
> To enter our Rome gates. I'th'peoples' name
> I say it shall be so. (3.3.93–105)

Sicinius, as usual, has sounded in this "sentencing" of Martius the same themes we have heard from him all along: that he is a minister of the people, that he speaks in the name of the people, that Martius wants to take away the power of the people. Sicinius, we know, does not care about the people, but Shakespeare shows how political rhetoric, contrived such as it is here, in its repetition and circulation is as powerful in its ability to destroy people as is Martius's sword on the battlefield. Two powerful institutions come into conflict in this scene: the military and the governing body. Although a Roman patrician was expected to do service in both, Martius finds honor in only one; the other, as Shakespeare presents it, affirms for Martius what he believes to be true of the political arena: it lacks honor. Martius cannot imagine himself in service to a Rome that requires dissembling.

With the people's cry "It shall be so, it shall be so! Let's away with him! / He's banish'd, and it shall be so" (3.3.106–107), Cominius tries to intervene, but he is silenced by Sicinius and Brutus and the shouts of the people. In this moment of triumph for the tribunes and the people against an old patrimonial form of government, Martius sees Rome for what it is, not for what he has imagined. Martius served an ideal of Rome, which favored the patricians over plebeians, military service over farming, devotion to parents and family over pursuing individual need. The people's "shall" ringing in his ears, Martius's response is expected. This time, however, his anger is directed not only at the tribunes, but also at the people.

> You common cry of curs! whose breath I hate
> As reek o'th'rotten fens, whose loves I prize
> As the dead carcasses of unburied men
> That do corrupt my air: I banish you! (3.3.120–23)

As he was before when he was surrounded by a group of Romans, Martius is alone. He is not less alone in Rome's gates than he was in Coriole's gates when he was abandoned by his troops. His "I banish you" suggests he alone is Roman. He goes on to warn them what their life will be like without a Roman like himself to defend them:

> And here remain with your uncertainty!
> Let every feeble rumour shake your hearts!
> Your enemies, with nodding of their plumes,
> Fan you into despair! (3.3.124–27)

He mocks their political voice and the power they feel it affords them:

> Have the power still
> To banish your defenders, till at length
> Your ignorance—which find not till it feels,
> Making but reservation of yourselves,
> Still your own foes—deliver you as most
> Abated captives to some nation
> That won you without blows! (3.3.127–33)

Martius knows that Rome needs its defenders, that action, not words, usually wins battles, a fact of life. And then as the tribunes have done, spoken in the name of the people, Martius speaks in the name of the city:

> Despising
> For you the city, thus I turn my back.
> There is a world elsewhere! (3.3.133–35)

Martius leaves the stage following his passionate remarks, with the cheers of the people, and their throwing their caps in the air. The hypocrisy of this visual display of approval by the people reinforces the hypocrisy of their verbal approval. An act earlier, the people show their approval of Martius's military glory in winning Corioles and being given the name Caius Martius Coriolanus in the same manner: shouting and throwing their caps. The plebeian triumph is capped by their shouting "The gods preserve our noble tribunes!" (3.3.143). The most ignoble of men are named noble by the people whom Sicinius and Brutus have deceived. Shakespeare ultimately shows at the close of Act Three a gullible, foolish patrician banished, and a gullible, foolish people their "own foes."

The great conflict that closes Act Three is followed by relative calm at the open of Act Four. The stage now just occupied by Martius, with family and friends, is a separation scene; the weeping of Volumnia and Virgilia at Martius's leaving Rome leads him to comfort them. He tells Volumnia to be courageous. "I shall be lov'd when I am lack'd" (4.1.15), he tells her, after she curses "all trades in Rome" with a "red pestilence" (4.1.13–14). To Virgilia, Cominius, and Menenius in turn, Martius offers gracious and kind words, indicating he will prosper. He leaves the stage, leaving the audience with the impression that Martius is noble and honorable. Scene Two brings the tribunes and an aedile to the stage; the aedile is told to disperse the people, as Martius is no longer in Rome, and the tribunes no longer need the people to ensure that Martius leaves. Sicinius suggests that now that their plot has succeeded, they should appear more humble to the nobles. The noble Volumnia, however, like her son, will have her say to the tribunes, whom she spies while they attempt to avoid her: "Oh, y'are well met: the hoarded plague o'th'gods / Requite your love!" (4.1.11–12). Menenius asks her to ignore them, but she stops the tribunes. Sicinius smartly asks, "Are you mankind?" (4.1.16). His contempt for her nobility is obvious, despite Volumnia's rude address. Volumnia's contempt for the tribunes is equally obvious. She asserts the nobility of the son that they have banished, and they mock her womanhood and sanity. The tribunes leave, Sicinius remarking, "Why stay we to be baited / With one that wants her wits?" (4.2.43–44). Volumnia can do nothing but curse them; Menenius asks her to "sup" with him, but she responds, "Anger's my meat: I sup upon myself / And so shall starve with feeding" (4.2.50–51). And as if this act of despair is noble, she tells Menenius that she will "lament . . . / In anger, Juno-like" (4.2.52–53). She and Virgilia leave the stage, with Menenius muttering "Fie, fie, fie," and the scene closes.

The third scene in Act Four is short, one in which a Volscian and Roman meet, and intelligence of Rome's vulnerability is passed on to the Volscian. The Roman, Nicanor, meets Adrian, the Volscian. Nicanor identifies himself as a Roman who works against Rome. The exchange between the two men anticipates the exchange we will shortly see between Martius and Aufidias.

After their exit from the stage, Martius appears, opening Scene Four. The hero is not wearing the garments of the Roman nobility or the trappings of a Roman warrior, but cloaked and disguised in *mean apparel.* He has gone to Antium, where he knows Aufidias resides after he left Corioles in disgust. Martius says aloud, "A goodly city is this Antium. City, / 'Tis I that made thy widows" (4.4.1–2). Discovering from a passing citizen that he is standing in front of the house in which he will find Aufidias, alone again, Martius reveals his thoughts on his banishment, which are cynical. He has come to believe friends fall out and become enemies over nothing, and enemies become friends over "some trick not worth an egg" (4.4.21). "My birthplace hate I, and my love's upon / This enemy town" (4.4.23–24). The last we saw of Martius, he was comforting his family and friends. Yet the seeds of his desire to revenge Rome might have begun with his shouting "I banish you" to the tribunes and Romans who rejected him. Martius is alone. His identity being rooted in his being a noble and honorable servant of Rome, Martius is no longer such. Thus, he is drawn to Aufidias, a determined soldier, a person with whom Martius feels he can identify. Switching loyalties is not like Martius, but in the prior scene, we saw that he is not the first Roman to do so. Rome has its problems.

Scene Five opens with three servingmen preparing a meal in the hearth area into which Martius enters. Thinking Martius a poor man looking for food, the servants attempt to talk him into leaving. Martius tells them that he is a gentleman, and expects gentle treatment. When that is not forthcoming, he begins to bully them. The exchange between members of this group is meant to be humorous, but it also shows how difficult it is for

Martius to communicate with his supposed inferiors. The servants, or "clowns," are verbally abused and roughed up by Martius, probably for the audience's amusement. The Globe audiences liked the clowns. When Aufidias is brought to him, we see then that not only do the clowns not recognize "nobility" when they see it, but that also Aufidias does not recognize the enemy he has fought so many times in battle. Martius is left to tell him, and in a speech of thirty-eight lines (4.5.66–102) identifies himself as man who has done to Aufidias "and to all the Volsces, / Great hurt and mischief" (4.5.67–68). Martius explains his banishment and offers his service to Aufidias and the Volsces. "Make my misery serve thy turn" (4.5.89), suggests Martius; he also offers his throat to Aufidias, to cut, if he would rather, as revenge.

Aufudias, in response, follows with thirty-six lines (4.5.102–36)[39] telling Martius how happy he is to meet him, for Aufidias, like Martius, has often thought of how he might take this formidable enemy in battle. "Let me twine / Mine arms about that body, where against / My grained ash an hundred times has broke"[40] (4.5.107–109), enthuses Aufidias. The presence of his foremost enemy moves Aufidias to tell Martius

Know thou first
I lov'd the maid I married; never man
Sigh'd truer breath; but that I see thee here,
Thou noble thing, more dances my rapt heart
Than when I first my wedded mistress saw
Bestride my threshold. (4.5.114–19)

The excitement generated by the aid Martius offers causes Aufidias to effuse in terms that conjure the homoerotic, not to mention impress upon us the pleasure these soldiers take in battle, in dominating the enemy.[41] Aufidias reveals to Martius

Thou hast beat me out
Twelve several times, and I have nightly since
Dreamt of encounters 'twixt thyself and me—
We have been down and together in my sleep,
Unbuckling helms, fisting each other's throat—
And wak'd half dead with nothing. (4.5.122–27)

Aufidias's dreams of dominating Martius should be a warning to Martius, even though Aufidias says that the only thing between them has been Rome. With Rome an enemy to Martius, too, Aufidias finds in Martius a partner in dominating other Romans. Martius for Aufidias at one time was Rome, and to conquer him would be to conquer Rome, which would bring him glory and honor in his own land. Without Martius as a threat, Rome in essence is conquered literally and metaphorically. From this moment, blinded by the desire to avenge himself, Martius is owned by Aufidias. He should see the envy Aufidias feels for him, but as Martius underestimated the tribunes' envy, he misunderstands Aufidias's envy as admiration. Welcomed to Antium, Martius is offered an army to lead against Rome and its territories. Ironically, as Leggat points out, Aufidias is the man who will reunite Martius with Rome, his home, his mother, his wife (204).

In the next, scene, presumably at the same time, the tribunes, who have entered the empty stage, note how happy the plebeians are, and in turn, how Menenius has "grown most kind" (4.6.11) to them. Menenius enters and greets them, and Sicinius tells him, "Your Coriolanus is not much miss'd" (4.6.13). Both tribunes insist on the rightness of their banishing Martius, with Brutus insisting,

> Caius Martius was
> A worthy officer i'th'war, but insolent
> O'ercome with pride, ambitious past all thinking,
> Self-loving. (4.6.29–32)

The hypocritical tribunes are at the height of their career, and as is often the case with the *de casibus* theme, it signals a reverse in fortune. An aedile brings the news that the Volscians are entering Rome's territories, which is confirmed by a messenger, and this brings Cominius to the stage, where he tells the tribunes that they "have made good work" (4.6.90) and that they are responsible for what will happen to Rome as a result. Martius, Cominius tells Menenius and the tribunes,

> is [the Volscians'] god. He leads them like a thing
> Made by some other deity than nature. (4.6.91–92)

The tribunes say they cannot be blamed, but Menenius blames them and the citizens, who now begin to enter the stage in fear. Menenius charges:

> You are they
> That made the air unwholesome when you cast
> Your stinking greasy caps in hooting at
> Coriolanus' exile. Now he's coming,
> . . . .

As many coxcombs
As you threw caps up will he tumble down,
And pay you for your voices. (4.6.130–37)

The voices and caps, sound and sight, collapse into one another as a symbol of ruin. The citizens begin to claim that when they banished Martius, they did so against their will. If this is the case, then it would seem the people had no voice at all, which is, after all, the chief complaint of Martius. The charges he laid against the people in Act One seem to be true, and in some historical accounts of Martius, he is very critical of the people. In this play, however, it is the tribunes whom Martius attacks, and until his banishment, Martius does not direct his attacks against representation so much against the people as he does the tribunes. The tribunes thus see their plot turn against them, the people indicating they were duped into banishing Martius. As the citizens leave the stage stating their regrets for their decision, the tribunes leave hoping that Martius is not leading the Volscian army against Rome, showing no regrets. The actors leaving the stage anticipate the next scene, in which Aufidias and his lieutenant enter. "Do they still fly to th'Roman?" (4.7.1) asks Aufidias, envious over the fact that the Volscian troops follow Martius as a god. Martius has been an exemplary military commander and consequently has supplanted Aufidias as leader. Martius's virtuous ways, as they have in the past, incur the envy of lesser men and in turn will lead to his ruin. Aufidias, moreover, believes Martius will be welcomed back to Rome "by sovereignty of nature" (4.7.35). Despite that part of Martius's character that led to his banishment, Aufidias knows that Martius "has a merit / To choke it in the utt'rance. So our virtues / Lie in th'interpretation of the time" (4.7.48–49). Under the circumstances, claims Aufidias, the Romans will remember Martius for his greatness and will wish him home, as the Roman citizens utter in 4.6. Martius counts on the Roman response, for once Martius has Rome, Aufidias will have Martius (4.7.57).

Caius Martius Coriolanus attempts to show himself most invulnerable in Act Five, although he possibly has never been more vulnerable, more human. As Scene One opens, Cominius is telling Menenius and the tribunes that Martius has refused his appeals to save Rome. The two tribunes are trying to talk Menenius into going to Martius, but Cominius has doubts. He says Martius "was a kind of nothing" (5.1.13). Cominius goes on to say, "I tell you, he does sit in gold, his eye / The gaoler to his pity. I kneel'd before him, / 'Twas very faintly he said 'Rise', dismiss'd me / Thus, with his speechless hand" (5.1.63–67).

Martius, who showed himself extremely fond of Cominius prior to his banishment, has steeled himself against one of his staunchest allies. Worse, he sends a letter to Cominius describing what he plans to do with Rome and on what conditions (5.1.68–69). Martius's silence conveys to Cominius that he is impenetrable, but Menenius thinks that if Martius is well-dined, perhaps his mood will be amenable to a visit by Menenius: "when we have stuff'd / These pipes and these conveyances of our blood / With wine and feeding, we have suppler souls / Than in our priest-like fasts" (5.1.53–56). Menenius, who told the fable of the belly in Act One, suggested the belly was the senate. The senate, he claimed, sent nourishment to other members of the body, kept them in working order. Will Menenius nourishing Martius remind Martius of what corporate order nourished him? Or will it remind Martius of what social corps banished him? Starved him?

Menenius's attempt to appeal to Martius in Act Five, Scene Two, fails. His arrogant patrician Roman pride leads him to brag to the Volscian watch that Martius will see him; not given entrance, Menenius pleads his case, claiming Martius would see him if he knew he were there. Martius comes upon the scene and sends Menenius away with a letter. Martius is trying to prove to Aufidias that he is loyal to the Volscians, and that Romans will not move him to spare Rome. He tells Aufidias that he wants the "Volscian lords" to know how "plainly he has borne this business [ignored Roman pleas]" (5.3.3–4). Aufidias agrees that Martius has been honest and honorable. The problem is that Aufidias does not care about Roman honor, and Martius has fooled himself into believing that a former enemy would share his Roman value system. Into Aufidias's and Martius's company come Volumnia, Virgilia, Valeria, and young Martius, to petition Martius to save Rome. Upon sight of them, Martius weakens his resolve, even as he tells himself "let it be virtuous to be obstinate" (5.3.26). As he observes each, he says, in a parallel to his talking himself into standing before the people in his gown of humility during his candidacy for consul, "Let the Volsces / Plough Rome and harrow Italy" (5.3.33–34).[42] Martius's true feelings when he sees his family leap out, as Martius's feelings always do, yet as soon as he gives himself away, he hurriedly follows with

> I'll never
> Be such a gosling to obey instinct, but stand
> As if a man were author of himself
> And knew no other kin. (5.3.34–37)[43]

Martius still struggles with his perception of strength as being linked to his masculinity. He is vulnerable to his feelings for his mother, his wife, and child, and like any human, he instinctively wants to forget his "honor" in assuring Aufidias and the Volscians that he will help them to Rome. He believes he can overcome instinct, however, if he hardens himself against the women. He imagines a man without a mother, "author of himself," believing that if he were lacking a link to woman through the womb, then he would be more a man.[44]

Martius, however, upon hearing the women speak, struggles mightily to be the man with whom he identifies as masculine. His family moves him to express feelings that he refuses to show Menenius or Cominius:

> Like a dull actor now
> I have forgot my part and I am out,
> Even to a full disgrace. Best of my flesh,
> Forgive my tyranny. (5.3.40–43)

Then, in a release of pent-up feelings, Martius turns to his wife, embracing and kissing her, telling her of his chasteness since their last meeting.

> O, a kiss
> Long as my exile, sweet as my revenge!
> Now by the jealous queen of heaven, that kiss
> I carried from thee, dear; and my true lip
> Hath virgin'd it e'er since. (5.3.44–48)

Martius leans heavily on his honor to help him control his feelings of vulnerability. In respect to his mother, he kneels, as required by a son to his mother. But in turn, she kneels, to the disturbance of Martius: the reversal of an ordered world as he knows it stirs in him thoughts of chaos:

> Then let the pebbles on the hungry beach
> Filip[45] the stars. Then let the mutinous winds
> Strike the proud cedars 'gainst the fiery sun,
> Murd'ring impossibility, to make
> What cannot be, slight work! (5.3.58–62)

Cleopatra could have said this, the emotions expressed are so freely hyperbolic. At the same time, the irony of Martius's position is too evident. Volumnia responds: "Thou art my warrior: / I holp to frame thee" (5.3.62–63). The control that Volumnia has exerted over her son for nearly his whole life once again begins to affect him. He turns cold, as the image of his greeting to Valeria indicates when his mother notes her presence:

Coriolanus Act 5, sc. 3. Pen and wash drawing by Joseph N. Paton, produced for the National Shakespeare 1888–89. By Permission of the Shakespeare Birthplace Trust.

> The noble sister of Publicola,
> The moon of Rome, chaste as the icicle
> That's curdied by the frost from purest snow
> And hangs on Dian's temple! (5.3.64–67)

Although Martius appears to be flattering Valeria, his thoughts are on cold natural phenomena: frost, snow, icicle, as if he were fighting the warmer emotions that would interfere with his course of action. He collects himself, and reminds the group that he will not grant any requests to keep his Volscian soldiers from "Rome's mechanics" (5.3.83). Volumnia ignores him, and in eighty-four lines appeals to Martius to consider the pain he brings his family, who must choose between their loyalty to him and to Rome, to his ignominy if he were to destroy Rome, and to the fact that to destroy Rome would be to destroy what nourished him.

Volumnia's speech to Martius, referred to as her "oration" in Plutarch (361), follows North's translation closely, the difference being that Shakespeare invokes the analogy of Rome as a body with greater frequency and force. For instance, in Plutarch, Volumnia warns her son: "thou shalt no soner marche forward to assault thy countrie, but thy foote shall tread upon thy mothers wombe that brought thee first into this world" (Brockbank 362). Shakespeare's Volumnia is more emphatic: "thou shalt no sooner / March to assault thy country than to tread—Trust to't, thou shalt not—on thy mother's womb / That brought thee to this world" (5.3.122–25). Without Shakespeare's having Volumnia interject with the phrase "Trust to't, thou shalt not," the two passages would be identical. Shakespeare's Volumnia is not just the parent who reminds Martius of the respect due Roman parents, as she is in Plutarch; she is the controlling force in Martius's life. Her commanding him "thou shalt not" is an imperative, not a plea, as if he were still an unruly youth. Much of what we have seen of Martius indicates an unruly nature, much of it grounded in his upbringing. His mother, as we have seen, has raised him to satisfy her longings for honor, glory, and fame. What Shakespeare brings out in Volumnia's oration is the parallel between Volumnia and Rome itself. Both are mothers that nourish their children to bring honor, glory, and fame to state and family. Both are feeding mothers: they feed their children and then feed on them.[46]

In the early phase of her oration, Volumnia reminds Martius of her and the family's agony over having to pray to the gods for a man who is "tearing / His countries bowels out" (5.3.102–103) with the fear he arouses. Volumnia as much as refers to herself as to Rome here, however, as her deep shame brings her pain. She emphasizes how difficult it is to pray for country and son when they are at odds: either "The country, our dear nurse" or Martius will win the impending battle (5.3.110). The nurse or "mother" is Rome and Volumnia herself. Volumnia reminds Martius that if he wins Rome, he will "triumphantly tread upon [his] countries ruin" or upon Rome, his mother. Volumnia, who earlier talked of Martius treading upon Tullus Aufidias, now attempts to move him with an image of his treading upon Rome, his mother. Virgilia speaks out, too, reminding Martius of her womb, of the child that she bore to keep the family name alive (5.3.125–27). Martius's son, not to be restrained, tells his father that he will not "tread" upon him: "I'll run away till I am bigger, but then I'll fight" (5.3.127–28). Young Martius is a portion of the body politic who plans to escape his father's fury. In that moment, we see in the two Martiuses the irony of being a man in Rome. Born to fight for the repressive mother, in the fight for escape it is implicit that escape will never come.

The following portion of Volumnia's orations makes appeals to male *virtus*. Volumnia mentions all the important words: "noble" (145, 154), "honour" (135, 149, 154, 164), and "duty" (167). Then she turns the focus back to herself:

> There's no man in the world
> More bound to's mother, yet here he lets me prate
> Like one i'th'stocks. Thou hast never in thy life
> Show'd thy deare mother any courtesy,
> When she, poor hen, fond of no second brood,
> Has cluck'd thee to the wars, and safely home,
> Loaden with honour. Say my request's unjust,
> And spurn me back, but if it be not so,
> Thou art not honest; and the gods will plague thee
> That thou restrain'st from me the duty which
> To a mother's part belongs. (158–68)

For his part, Martius has remained silent, which is noted in the text by Volumnia's asking, "Why dost not speak?" (153). In front of her son, family, and Volscians, Volumnia finds herself practicing that art of cajoling that she wished her son could have used with the tribunes and people in Act Three. Her rhetorical arsenal is loaded, however. Shamed by her son, cliché, metaphor, hyperbole, and a threat flow forth as Volumnia freights her son with emotional appeals. Volumnia is Rome: Martius's duty is to Rome. He will agree to a peace between the Volscians and Rome: no one loses, except Martius.

Volumnia's speech is partly from Plutarch, as is Martius's finally taking his mother's hand and saying, "O mother, mother! / What have you done" (5.3.182–83) and as for her son, "Most dangerously you have with him prevail'd, / If not most mortal to him" (5.3.188–89). Volumnia is never heard from after this moment. She is later seen in Act Five, Scene Five, walking with Virgilia and Valeria across the stage in triumph. The scene parallels her son's earlier triumphant entry into Rome after he had taken Corioles. She is treated with honor, and ironically appears the soldier that she never herself could be. What Volumnia thinks of her son, of his fate, we do not know. As the feeding mother, she is sated. Gail Kern

Paster says that Martius's "decision to spare Rome and die—in a way, to starve with feeding—reveals the community to be in truth the mother who eats her children."[47]

What is left of Act Five is Aufidias's treachery. Envious over the success Martius has had with Volscian troops, even the commoners, who willingly follow him to battle, Aufidias's hostility toward Martius can no longer be borne by him. The Roman threat now diminished, Aufidias no longer needs Martius's service. He gathers conspirators, and they plot to kill Martius. Aufidias has also sent a message to the lords of Antium suggesting that Martius has cheated the city out of material gain from the war. When Martius arrives triumphant at Antium, he is accompanied by the commoners, who ironically like him. He has actually brought great wealth and peace to Antium, but just as the tribunes were able to do in Rome, Aufidias jumps in and accuses Martius of being a traitor (5.6.85). Surprised, Martius says, "Traitor? How now!" to which Aufidias responds, "Ay, traitor, Martius!"

Martius is surprised by being called by his Roman name. Aufidias again, "Ay, Martius, Caius Martius! Dost thou think / I'll grace thee with that robbery, thy stol'n name / Coriolanus, in Corioles?" (5.6.88–90). Martius never asked for the name. For his service to Rome, he is given a name. He wanted honor. The name, indeed, marks him, and prepares him for his life among the Volscians. When Martius is called his Roman name by Aufidias, a name most like the god Mars, he is struck by what he is: a Roman. To the Volscians, he has always been an enemy, and even though he has acted in their welfare and for their honor, his past deeds against them are easy to recall. Aufidias charges that Martius has been weak, by giving up Rome "at his nurse's tears" (97). Martius says, "hear'st thou, Mars?" (101) as he speaks to the god Mars about this insult. Nastily Aufidias retorts, "Name not the god, thou boy of tears!" (5.6.101).

At the hearing of "boy," Martius is seen to be the Martius we remember in Rome: a man who would not brook being called a boy, a man who spent years in service proving he was no boy, but a man. To Aufidias, he can only rage: "Measureless liar, thou hast made my heart / Too great for what contains it. 'Boy'! O slave!" (5.6.102–103). Order is returning to Martius's life. Aufidias is not a Roman, not a great warrior. He is an enemy, an opportunist, who shares none of Martius's ideas of warriorhood. Although a lord attempts to intervene, Martius offers himself to the people: "Cut me to pieces, Volsces, men and lads, / Stain all your edges on me. Boy! False hound!" (5.6.111–112). Martius would rather be dead than be called a boy or a traitor. To enrage his supportive acquaintances, Martius reminds them of how he devastated their city. "I / Flutter'd your

Volscians in Corioles. / Alone I did it. Boy!" (5.6.114–116). A boy, thinks Martius, could not take a city alone. When another lord tries to quiet Aufidias, the conspirators and people call for Martius's death, and before the nobles can gain control, Martius is slain. Tullus Aufidias stands on him, a perversion of the order in which Volumnia claimed for Martius in Act One, Scene Two. Envy of Martius led to his banishment, and envy of his leadership skills leads to his death in Antium.

In the call for his mutilation, Martius imagines himself in fragments. Like the fragments he calls the Roman plebeians in Act One, Scene One, Martius invokes the image of the fragmented body politic.

NOTES

1. Maurice Charney, "The Dramatic Use of Imagery in Shakespeare's Coriolanus," *English Literature History* 23 (1956), p. 183.

2. Stanley Cavell, "Who Does the Wolf Love?: Reading *Coriolanus*," *Representations* 3 (1983), p. 5, sees Martius from another, not unrelated perspective. What Martius "incessantly hungers for . . . is not to hunger, not to desire, that is, not to be mortal."

3. D. A. Traversi, *An Approach to Shakespeare* (Garden City, NY: Doubleday, 1956), p. 219.

4. The term *voices* occurs forty-one times in the play, points out Norman Rabkin, "Coriolanus: The Tragedy of Politics," *Shakespeare Quarterly* 17 (1966), p. 205, indicating how significant an issue to Martius and the citizen is the right to representation.

5. Günter Grass, *The Plebeians Rehearse the Uprising*, trans. Ralph Manheim (London: Secker and Warburg, 1967), pp. xiii–xiv.

6. An excellent article arguing that Caius Martius's downfall is not because of his pride is Dean Frye's "Commentary in Shakespeare: The Case of *Coriolanus*" in *Shakespeare Studies* 1 (1965): 105–17.

7. Rabkin, "Coriolanus," pp. 205–206, says that for Martius, "Rome is an idea," and Martius honors that idea. His system of honor is based upon his idea of Rome, yet "paradoxically," Rome readily relieves itself of its most honorable member. The idea of Rome and Rome, however, are not the same, which is the point that Shakespeare makes.

8. Quoted in Anabelle Patterson, *Shakespeare and the Popular Voice* (New York: Blackwell, 1989), pp. 42–43. Published in 1615, the account from which I quote is by an eyewitness to the Kett uprising, Richard Woods, who was not sympathetic to the poor. It was printed after *Coriolanus*; however, it represents a rhetoric familiar long before. Patterson, p. 41, claims that it is in texts such as Woods that the idea of the peasants having rights was one long in circulation and appealed to during times of stress upon the poor population.

9. Ibid.

10. Andrew Gurr, "Coriolanus and the Body Politic," *Shakespeare Survey* 28 (1975), pp. 63–64.

11. Ibid., pp. 64–65.

12. Rabkin, "Coriolanus," p. 197, claims that the citizens present themselves as "ugly enough to throw our sympathies to Martius," with their staves and talk of killing Martius. Their suffering, though, is evident in the passages that follow.

13. G. Wilson Knight, *The Imperial Theme* (London: Methuen, 1965), p. 163, remarks that Martius makes use of images that contrast weak to strong, the plebeians being the weak, and he, the strong. It is Martius's habit in general to look at the world from a limited perspective, as would a person who had not yet matured psychologically or intellectually. He has ordered his world around a system of contrasts: patrician/not patrician, hard-working/lazy, wealthy/poor, etc.

14. Robin Headlam Wells, *Shakespeare, Politics, and the State* (London: Macmillan, 1986), p. 50.

15. Ibid., p. 51.

16. Maurice Charney, p. 184, notes that Martius uses images whose "function is illustrative rather than expressive." Maurice Charney, "The Dramatic Use of Imagery in Shakespeare's Coriolanus," *English Literary History* 23 (1956).

17. Ibid., p. 184, thinks Martius lacks reflectiveness or inwardness as a way to explain why the characters and play are not appealing to audiences.

18. Precepts or proverbs from the sixteenth century can be found in Morris Tilley's *Dictionary of the Proverbs in England in the Sixteenth and Seventeenth Centuries* (New York: AMS, 1950).

19. Carol M. Sicherman, "Coriolanus: The Failure of Words," *English Literary History* 39 (1972), p. 197. Ibid., p. 198, also asserts that Martius has "logorrhea." When he is around the patricians, his speech is "controlled," but around the plebeians, Martius cannot form full sentences, breaks off in cursing, or fails to complete a thought.

20. It is probably true that Martius invests his words with meaning, but it is equally true that it is a meaning he understands as a truth when he utters them. It is doubtful that he ever means to be untruthful. In his introduction to "*Coriolanus* and the Failure of Performatives," in *English Literary History* 63 (1996), John Plotz, p. 810, summarizes a critical stance taken by some, that "[a]ll the characters in *Coriolanus* are aware, underneath, that the linguistic games they are playing are fraudulent, that their talk is half to deceive others and half to keep themselves comfortably numb to their own motives: only Coriolanus says out loud what others keep under their hats."

21. D. A. Traversi, *The Roman Plays* (Stanford, CA: Stanford UP, 1963), p. 210, finds "the people express their grievances with reasoned moderation," a point sometimes overlooked by critics who are quick to argue that Shakespeare showed the plebeians as mob-like.

22. As Emrys Jones, *The Origins of Shakespeare* (Oxford: Oxford UP, 1977), p. 59, comments, the tribunes, not Aufidias, are Martius's antagonists, men who

are not unlike the "Caiaphuses and Annases" of the mystery cycles, those men who urged Pilate to punish Jesus with death.

23. Jay Halio, "*Coriolanus.* Shakespeare's Drama of Reconciliation," *Shakespeare Studies* 6 (1970), p. 293, observes that "despite his obvious pride, surely here is Coriolanus' implicit recognition that he is not a god, but a man, subject to human diseases and decay." The people "represent the image of starved humanity," says Halio, p. 293, the condition Martius attempts to transcend.

24. See Bernard J. Paris, *Character as a Subversive Force in Shakespeare: The History and Roman Plays* (London: Associated UP, 1991), p. 167.

25. Anne Barton, "Livy, Machiavelli, and Shakespeare's Coriolanus," *Shakespeare Survey* 38 (1985), p. 116, believes that Shakespeare probably read Livy in school, several decades before it was translated into English by Holland.

26. Literally, once enemy men are slain, sexual access to the women will not be hampered.

27. Sicherman, "Coriolanus: The Failure," p. 197, adds that when he is emotional, Martius curses, a habit he has learned from his mother, who also curses when she is emotional.

28. "Carbuncle" is "any kind of red, translucent, fiery stone" (Philip Brockbank, ed., *Coriolanus. The Arden Shakespeare* [London: Methuen, 1976], p. 130).

29. Ann C. Christensen, p. 302, in her essay on Martius's antagonistic feelings toward domesticity or home life, points out that the items he mentions the soldiers taking are domestic items; Martius wants their thoughts on battle, not home, as home represents surrender to that which Martius longs to escape. Ann C. Christensen, "The Return of the Domestic in *Coriolanus*," *Studies in English Literature* 37 (1997).

30. This line is variously given to Martius or to the plebeians. The *Folio* assigns it to Martius, but the Arden editors have decided upon giving the line to the soldiers (Brockbank, *Coriolanus*, p. 138).

31. Here the meaning of doffing of caps is a sign of respect (Brockbank, *Coriolanus*, p. 155, n. 68).

32. Charles Wells, *The Wide Arch* (New York: St. Martin's, 1994), p. 96.

33. Thomas Sorge, "The Failure of Orthodoxy in Coriolanus," in *Shakespeare Reproduced: The Text in History and Ideology*, ed. Jean E. Howard and Marion F. O'Connor (New York: Methuen, 1987), p. 235, thinks that the organic metaphor of the human body as body politic so popular with ruling governments in Tudor and Jacobean England should be one exploited by Martius. The showing of his wounds and body is important to the notion of Martius's being part of the body politic.

34. Shakespeare has compressed into several dramatic scenes what occurs over the course of a few days, historically. The tribunes in Plutarch's narrative of Martius are warned by the patricians that executing Martius would not be lawful or just.

35. See Sorge, "The Failure of Orthodoxy," p. 237.

36. The exchange between Martius and Volumnia does not occur in Plutarch.

37. In his discussion of the way that the public discourse in Martius's Rome is antithetical to Martius's belief that language should express the truth, Plotz, "*Coriolanus* and the Failure," p. 816, believes that "Coriolanus's reaction to his mother's speech can only strengthen the case for our seeing his self-consuming tragedy as a reaction to a world full of 'roted' and manipulative speech. Coriolanus cries out against the 'harlotry' of unrooted language in some of the most moving passages in the play. Three times his mother tries to shame him into lying to the plebs so he can hold on to power. Two times he refuses, and finally, near heartbreak—those who have just discovered that they are bastards in the truth are always heartbroken—he replies:

> Pray be content.
> Mother, I am going to the market-place.
> Chide me no more. I'll mountebank their loves,
> Cog their hearts from them and come home beloved
> Of all the trades in Rome. (3.2.132–36)

38. What prerogative is not clear, but Brockbank, *Coriolanus*, writes that Shakespeare is referencing North's "ancient precedence of the people's verdict" (229).

39. This speech does not occur in Plutarch.

40. The "grained ash" is likely a lance.

41. Ralph Berry, "Sexual Imagery in Coriolanus," *Studies in English Literature* 13 (1973), p. 309, thinks that the sexual imagery in the play emphasizes the relationship between sex and war in the minds of Coriolanus and Aufidias. Dominance is what both men seek. Madelon Sprengnether, "Annihilating Intimacy in *Coriolanus*," *Coriolanus: Critical Essays*, ed. David Wheeler (New York: Garland, 1995), p. 191, argues that "both men use the rhetoric of heterosexual passion to express intensity of feeling for another man." Coriolanus's dominance over Aufidias on the battlefield has been won, so he feels no threat from Aufidias.

42. In Act Two, Scene Three, Martius, waiting for the next group of citizens, says, "Rather than fool it so, / Let the high office and honour go / To one that would so thus" (2.3.120–22).

43. Similarly, Martius builds his resolve once he considers the consequences: "I am half through, / The one part suffer'd, the other will I do" (2.3.122–23).

44. Sprengnether, "Annihilating Intimacy," p. 194, sees in this passage Martius "severing himself from his mother."

45. To strike.

46. Gail Kern Paster, *The Idea of the City in the Age of Shakespeare* (Athens: U of Georgia P, 1985), p. 89.

47. Ibid., p. 89.

4

THEMES

Themes in *Coriolanus* are mostly related to how an individual negotiates political and social structures, cultural values, and personal and social relationships. Revenge, individualism, and social stability, themes common to Shakespeare's other tragedies, to be sure, are evident in *Coriolanus*. Specific to this play are other themes that single it out: the dominant mother, the struggle between classes, and the Roman city. None of the themes stand alone in this play, for Martius's desire to revenge his banishment from Rome is linked to his individual ideas about governance—which are not accepted by the people—who banish him. Martius's mother, a fancy-driven Roman matron, indoctrinates Martius into the Roman ideal of the patrician class: militarism as a means to glorifying the family name and as a prerequisite to statecraft. Martius's nature is suited to war, but not to tactful policy-making between various members of the Roman social order. Volumnia, like the city of Rome itself, exploits Martius's martial prowess, but when he shows signs of not wishing to lose his selfhood to statecraft, he is no longer useful or necessary to either Volumnia or Rome.

To revenge his banishment, Martius wants to destroy Rome, an act of treason. Othello's revenge on Desdemona for her perceived infidelity does not constitute treason, a problem Hamlet shares with Martius. If Hamlet has been misled by the ghost of his father, who wants his death revenged, Hamlet's killing Claudius would be treason. If Martius destroys Rome, the city to which he owes allegiance, treason is the result. In neither play, however, do revenge and potential treason dominate. It is the conflict between the hero and community norms that thrusts itself forward. Thus, while revenge is a theme in *Coriolanus*, it serves more to create a scenario in which Martius will be completely subdued by his mother, Volumnia, and by his motherland, Rome. If Martius had not threatened revenge on Rome, then Volumnia would have had no reason to appeal to her son's better judgment. Thus, the revenge theme, while present, serves as a plot device, one which allows a number of other themes to be explored on the way to the hero's likely fall.

Martius's tragedy is similar to Shakespeare's other tragedies, in which the hero's individual appetites, desires, needs, or wants assert themselves over community standards or norms, and, in turn, leave the community in chaos. In his discussion of Shakespeare's Jacobean tragedy, Maynard Mack sees in the "heroic mood" a hero whose desire to be an individual, to be "resolute, autonomous, and free," is at odds with the desire to be "realistic, adaptable, and secure" (29). Martius is this hero: he is easily Shakespeare's most virtuous hero. Except for his elitism and short temper, Martius lacks a malevolent nature. He fights and kills others as duty requires on the battlefield, but off the battlefield, we see Martius wielding his tongue, not his sword. Martius does not lust for power or wealth—only his due in battle spoils (1.9.37–40); he is sexually chaste (5.3.47–48). Martius does not envy others. He is modest in body and mind (1.9.41–49 and 2.2.135–38). Martius is charged with pride by characters in the play and by critics, but pride is not quite the case. Martius wants abstractions: honor, glory, respect—Roman virtues.

As a hero, Martius is as resolute to succeed in his military campaigns as he is to prevent the plebeians from gaining more voice in government. Martius is not adaptable. He dislikes change. Autonomy might be his single greatest desire, but the Roman ideal of *pietas* allows no room for autonomy. Banished from his community, Martius is most alone, yet most free. When his mother comes to the Volscian camp to plead for Rome's safekeeping, Martius's autonomy is swallowed up in his mother's rhetoric of devotion and fidelity to state and family.

Despite Bradley's claim that "[a] political conflict is never the centre of interest in Shakespeare's plays" (*"Coriolanus"* 4), from the beginning, the play has been exploited by other dramatists and interpreted by critics as a political play. Bradley goes on to admit that the political theme in *Coriolanus* is "very prominent" (*"Coriolanus"* 4), yet he cautions that critics and others "should feel it extremely hazardous to ascribe to [Shakespeare] any political feelings at all," and that it is "ridiculous to pretend to certainty on the subject" (*"Coriolanus"* 5).[1]

How Shakespeare felt about the social ranks or political justice in England during his lifetime certainly cannot be known by his plays, and actually, it need not be known to interpret the play.[2] Unlike later dramatists who saw his play as supporting one political stance or another, using it to send a political message to audiences, Shakespeare does not reveal his thoughts on Jacobean politics. Alexander Leggat suggests that Shakespeare was not so much interested in political structures and how they come to be as in observing how people responded to the political world in which they lived (238). For instance, Martius's response to the empowering of the lower classes compared to Menenius's is notable in that Menenius feels none of the anxiety borne by Martius over the tribunes' position of representing the plebeians. Shakespeare, to be sure, is following Plutarch's narrative, and Plutarch does show a Menenius and Martius who respond differently. All in all, though, Shakespeare shows a response to class conflict, not an analysis of class conflict, nor does he introduce his text, as the first three recorded plays on the Coriolanus theme in England did, as a means "to legitimate a favored social order."[3]

Even if Shakespeare is ambiguous about his politics, the play invites us to consider political and economic social structures that lead to conflict between those whose needs are being met and those whose needs are not. Shakespeare's own England was experiencing growing pains as a nation, and some of the material in Plutarch and Shakespeare seems to address similar political and social concerns, so it is not unreasonable to assume that perhaps Shakespeare was directing us to examine his political world situated within a fictional past. Clifford Davidson remarks that "the play is ordered around a central question: what is the proper relationship between an individual and his state?" (264). Davidson thinks perhaps Shakespeare, like others of the period, appreciated historical narratives for what they illuminated about current events (Davidson 264). Plutarch's narrative of Caius Martius includes a fable that draws attention to the function of members in a social order, which Shakespeare includes in his tragedy (264).

What was Shakespeare's England like? King James I, absolutist in ideology,[4] sat on the English throne when *Coriolanus* was written. An aristocratic monarchy ruled, and the rest were the ruled. Michael Bristol compares the ruled in Shakespeare's England to the plebeians in *Coriolanus*, referencing them as the "cognates in the early modern period—Shakespeare's 'citizens' "—"a complex ensemble of producing classes." The plebeians are a "political entity, nominally excluded from the function of rule but nevertheless a collective agent within the dynamic of political life" (209). Without a body to rule, James has no job, nor do

Rome's senators. The English, it seems, would be ruled, but only if they could tolerate the rule. Patterson introduces one concept the English had of themselves in an account that shows they believed, at root, that even if there were a class system in England, all, rich and poor alike, had a right to the riches of Nature:

> Shall they, as they have brought hedges about common Pastures, inclose with their intolerable lusts also, al the commodities and pleasure of this life, which Nature, the Parent of us all, would have common, and bringeth foorth every day for us, as well as for them? . . . Nature hath provided for us, as well as for them, hath given us a body, and a soule, and hath not envied us to her things. While we have the same forme, and the same condition of birth together with them, why should they have a life so unlike unto ours, and differ so farre from us in calling? We see now that it is come to extremeties, wee will also proove extremitie: rend downe hedges, fill up ditches, make way for everie man into the common pasutre. . . . Neither will we suffer ourselves any more to bee pressed with such burthens against our willes, nor endure so great shame, as living out our dayes under such inconveniences, wee should leave the Commonwealth unto our posterities, mourning, and miserable, and much worse than we received it of our fathers. (42–43)[5]

Like the Roman plebeians, the English rebelled. The Midlands Insurrection in May 1607 was an attempt by peasants in Northamptonshire and neighboring counties to level the enclosures on arable land. Enclosures prevented farming, and with a corn dearth at hand, the peasants wanted to use the land for planting and harvest. The lack of tools needed to fulfill the peasants' aim or to protect themselves from gentry who stopped them led to the insurrection's being put down. Some of the insurrectionists were executed, although there was talk of "redress" for the peasants.[6] In 1608, evidence of grain dearths and requests for measures to be taken to distribute grain at fair prices suggest that the government attempted some form of redress.[7] The parallels between a grain dearth in Plutarch's biography of Caius Martius and in Shakespeare's immediate past are difficult to ignore, especially when we consider what Shakespeare drew from Plutarch. As E. C. Pettet reminds us, Plutarch's plebeians had two complaints that wanted redress: usurers and grain dearths. Shakespeare keeps the grain dearths as the central complaint of the plebeians in his play (37). Thus, it appears that local politics might have influenced what Shakespeare drew or cut from his source. Whatever the case, the document that was left for audiences to read, written as it was in a particular cultural milieu, a particular historical moment, lends itself to political readings.

Although the earliest dramatic interpretations of *Coriolanus* were political in intent, they were not analyses or critiques of political structures, as we have seen, nor have "political readings" of the text always revealed much about the play's politics; sometimes readings reveal more about the reader. As Stanley Cavell writes, "a political reading is apt to become fairly predictable once you know whose side the reader is taking, that of the patricians or that of plebeians" (2). Whatever the case, close readings of the text can provide evidence to support a variety of claims about Shakespeare's politics, the play's politics, or even the critic's politics. For instance, Pettet believes that Shakespeare's mob in *Coriolanus* "was no where else . . . shown so emphatically and continuously in an unfavorable light" and that Shakespeare's depiction of the plebeians was a "worse picture" than that described by his source, Plutarch. Pettet's belief thus implies that we are to see Shakespeare as viewing the plebeians in an unsympathetic light.[8] Roy Walker thinks that Shakespeare "probes a deeper rottenness, the baseness of the people themselves, who banish the best from Rome and thereby destroy Rome from below" (291). On the other hand, Anne Barton claims that *Coriolanus* "is unique in the canon for the tolerance and respect it accords an urban citizenry" (117). Barton cites the instance of the plebeians at the play's start who show themselves capable of controlling their own rebellion, not to mention capable of reasoning the politics of their discord. Their motivations for mob action are not revenge, but hunger (117).

Looking into which light the citizens are cast suggests we are looking at them from a center of power that would put them on the margins, as if Shakespeare's point of view was from that of the senate or aristocracy. Actually, the hero is not presented in the best light either, his puerile bullying of the people indicating a rank immaturity. By the end of the play, the hero is dead, the people no better or worse off, and the aristocratic order still intact. The class conflict represented by the people versus Martius is ended not by the people but by enemies to Roman citizens. A third party steps in and puts to rest an antagonism between the two. What is interesting about the ending is that Martius is silenced, not the people, whose right to a voice he reviled.

The antagonism, although not politically motivated, was rooted in political ideology. Martius believed in one kind of Rome, the people in another. As Patricia Meszaros sees the play, written as it was during a time of sociopolitical change in England, it presents a "vision" of how "political history—the fate of the *polis*, and tragedy—the fate of the individual—are interrelated" (274).[9] Meszaros points out that the word *state* is used at least twice as many times as it was in other plays. By the time James had ascended the throne, Meszaros asserts, England had become a state; the "The Roman state in the play was not the medieval *respublica* or the body politic of the familiar 'Elizabethan World Picture,' but the political entity described by Machiavelli and accepted as reality by Bacon" (Meszaros 275). Meszaros's reference to the Elizabethan world picture is to E.M.W. Tillyard's book of that title, in which Tillyard argues that Shakespeare's contemporaries believed in a world order that paralleled the natural order, that of the cosmos and the sublunar world. That an "ideal order animat[ed] the earthly order," says Tillyard, was a collective mindset, and there was a real fear of "chaos" if this order were disturbed (16). No doubt, Shakespeare's characters express fears of chaos or confusion that are the consequence of treason, murder, or usurpation, for instance, but by the time *Coriolanus* is written, a change in attitude appears to be occurring. This last Shakespearean tragedy, it might be noted, does not reference the cosmos or fate as a sign of confusion to come. *Coriolanus* begins with Rome already in a state of confusion.

It is this state against which Martius stands alone, isolated, clinging to an "outdated ideal" of Rome no longer accepted by the play's Romans or the Jacobean audience. Meszaros believes that "Marcius lives by a system in which human nature is an integral part of a Great Nature encompassing both *polis* and *cosmos*; the other characters live by a system which makes of politics a science answerable only to the necessity of maintaining the state and concerned with human qualities only as they are relevant to that end" (277).

Ordering a social group on the lines of natural order or rank is a theme examined in the play, but the play seems primarily to show what is wrong with such an analogy. The organic metaphor of the body politic as related in the fable of the belly, which is told at the play's beginning by Menenius, is recalled throughout the play by characters who differ in their political ideology. Popular during the Tudor and early Stuart periods was the analogy of the body to the political organization of a social order. When the First Citizen interrupts Menenius's tale with a description of the body politic as he has come to know it, with the "kingly crown'd head," "the vigilant eye," "the counsellor heart," "the arm our soldier," "our steed the leg," "the tongue our trumpeter," the First Citizen is letting Menenius know that he is familiar with an old concept. According to David Hale, the metaphor is "descended from John of Salisbury" (198).

Hale questions whether or not the analogy is useful in providing a "traditional standard of political morality by which we may judge the characters and their deeds" (199). It appears not, as it is interpreted by Martius and the tribunes in different ways.

Martius's membership in this polis or community is also shaped by ideals of masculinity. Rome, a patriarchal society, is rooted in a masculinist ethos from its start. The legends and myths of Rome reveal a culture constructed on male aggression, a warrior ethos, which subsequently is adopted as an ethos for living that will ensure the stability of the state, the Roman *virtus*. Included is a devotion not only to the state, but also to the family, to parents, wives, and children. Tensions between the self and social relations arise when anxieties about masculinity persist. This is particularly true of Caius Martius, who wants all to know that he is a man, not a boy. He dies, in a rage over being called a boy, a signal that his sense of identity was overly engaged in the masculinist *virtus*. Madelon Sprengnether cites Robert Stoller on object-relations theory, which asserts that from birth, a boy "is endangered by the primary, profound, primeval oneness with mother" that ever lives within the male child. Primeval oneness threatens to return at any moment in the person's life (180). Thus, Sprengnether says of Caius that "barriers to intimacy . . . stem from the hero's anxieties regarding the figure of a mother/lover who threatens the annihilation of his identity, a condition he both desires and fears" (188).

NOTES

1. John Palmer, *Political Characters of Shakespeare* (London: Macmillan, 1961), p. 334, also finds Shakespeare taking an "indifferent" position toward politics in his plays.

2. Critics, it seems, have blurred the distinction between Shakespeare's personal politics and the politics presented in the play. Granted, we do not need to know Shakespeare's feelings about commoners having a voice in government matters or the divine right of kings, but it is probably fair to conclude as Robin Headlam Wells, *Shakespeare, Politics, and the State* (London: Macmillan, 1986), p. 6, does, that Shakespeare probably had a mistrust of "a feckless and indecisive populace" such as the one found in *Coriolanus*.

3. John Ripley, *Coriolanus on Stage in England and America, 1609–1994* (Madison, Fairleigh Dickinson UP, 1998), p. 54, refers to Nahum Tate's "rework[ing] the play as a Tory tract" and to John Dennis who "rewrote the piece as Whig propaganda" and James Thomson's, whose is "Whig in spirit."

4. This point of view is argued by Paul Cefalu in " 'The End of Absolutism':

Shakespeare's *Coriolanus* and the Consensual Nature of the Early Modern State," *Renaissance Forum* 4 (2000).

5. The account refers to Robert Kett's 1549 Norfolk uprising, which occurred before the Midlands in 1607.

6. E.C. Pettett, "Coriolanus and the Midlands Insurrection of 1607," *Shakespeare Survey* 3 (1950), p. 34.

7. On June 2, 1608, a proclamation was made for preventing and remedying the dearth of grain and other victuals. Printed in Great Britain Public Record Office, *Calendar of State Papers, Domestic Series, of the Reigns of Edward VI, Mary, Elizabeth [and James I] 1547–1625*, 12 vols., ed. Robert Lemon (Nendeln, Liechtenstein: Kraus Reprint, 1967), 8:437.

8. Pettet, "Coriolanus and the Midlands Insurrection," p. 38. Roy Walker, "The Northern Star: An Essay on the Roman Plays," *Shakespeare Quarterly* 4 (1951), p. 291, wrote that "in *Coriolanus* Shakespeare probes a deeper rottenness, the baseness of the people themselves, who banish the best from Rome and thereby destroy Rome from below. Shakespeare at once shows through now familiar imagery that the revolt of the mob is treason against the divine-natural order."

9. H. J. Oliver, "Coriolanus as Tragic Hero," *Shakespeare Quarterly* 10 (1959), p. 55, makes a similar point when he writes the play presents the problem of an aristocrat unwilling to make the necessary "compromises" to live in a democratic or near-democratic society.

5

CRITICAL APPROACHES

Shakespearean criticism began as early as the late seventeenth century, when adaptations of the plays began to appear on the Restoration stage. Nahum Tate, John Dryden, and John Dennis, for instance, all modified Shakespeare's text's to suit neoclassical ideas about drama, and those adaptations undoubtedly figured in the way that the earliest editors approached Shakespeare's *Folio* and quartos.[1] Similarly, as a tragedy, *Coriolanus* from the start drew the attention of critics for the ways that it did or did not meet criteria for neoclassical tragedy. Dryden, one of Shakespeare's earliest critics, thought Shakespeare's habit of allowing actions to extend over longer periods than allotted for staging them was a fault,[2] but only because the neoclassicists thought the unities of time, place, and action were important in the writing of a tragedy.[3] The impulse to judge the tragedies against classical or Greek paradigms remained strong, although interest in Shakespearean character took shape by the end of the eighteenth century, which took criticism in a new direction. Also, regarding the play as a literary text, not only a theatrical text, introduced a critical tradition that has dominated twentieth-century criticism of Shakespeare. Within that tradition, approaches to the tragedies include bibliographical, new critical, Marxist, historical, Jungian, psychoanalytical, structuralist, deconstructionist, new historicist, cultural materialist, and feminist/gender. *Coriolanus* is distinguished by the interest in its political theme in most critical treatments, an interest which has been consistently true of the text since it was first adapted. Thus, Marxist, historicist, new historicist, feminist, and cultural materialist critics contribute much to the criticism. Interrogation of the genre and tragic characterization became popular early in the twentieth century, as did psychoanalysis of Martius's relationships with his mother or with Aufidias, or even with the plebeians.

GENRE

A common twentieth-century introduction to an essay on *Coriolanus* is that it is not very popular, but that may have been because of misperceptions of the play's purpose or because of critical biases. A. C. Bradley, one of the most influential critics on Shakespearean tragedy,[4] did not rank *Coriolanus* among the four tragedies that he named great: *Hamlet*, *Macbeth*, *Othello*, and *Lear*, even though all five heroes share qualities that Bradley described as "tragic traits" (20). Of the tragic characters in general, Bradley suggested that they

> were made of the stuff we find within ourselves and within the persons who surround them. But, by an intensification of the life which they share with others, they are raised above them; and the greatest are raised so far that, if we fully realise all that is implied in their words and actions, we become conscious that in real life we have known scarcely any one resembling them. Some, like Hamlet and Cleopatra, have genius. Others, like Othello, Lear, Macbeth, Coriolanus, are built on the grand scale; and desire, passion, or will attains in them a terrible force. In almost all we observe a marked one-sidedness, a predisposition in some particular direction; a total incapacity, in certain circumstances, of resisting the force which draws in this direction; a fatal tendency to identify the whole being with one interest, object, passion, or habit of mind. This, it would seem, is, for Shakespeare, the fundamental tragic trait. (20)

No doubt, post-Bradley, the four greats have garnered critical attention and stage space not afforded *Coriolanus*; by Bradley's own definition of a Shakespearean tragic hero, Coriolanus is particularly paradigmatic. He is a fearless, incredibly capable soldier; he serves the Roman state with unusual integrity. Martius's patrician elitism dominates his attitude toward the plebeians, as it is a "habit of mind." Caius Martius Coriolanus, to be sure, possessed the fundamental tragic trait. Yet in Shakespeare's last two Roman plays, Bradley notes a lack of evil that can be found in the "great four" (82–84). Had Coriolanus destroyed Rome, he would have provoked more terror in his audience and thus would have been a character more like Macbeth or Othello (82–84). That is not the case.

Bradley's paradigm for tragic character is of great importance because it was an effort by a critic to look for common elements in construction of tragic character in one of Shakespeare's genres to see if a pattern emerged, one that might be useful in interpreting the text. Yet the paradigm ends up limiting the tragedies to four, rather than to the whole body. Seven decades later, Maynard Mack examined the Jacobean tragedies as a group, of which *Coriolanus* is the last, and found some common internal features: a hero who is an "overstater," "a hyperbolist," is the first Mack defines (23–25). A "foil" or opposing voice to the overstater appears to be a feature of the tragedies according to Mack; the foil's voice is antithetical to that of the hero, either in its plainness or colloquial manner, and it usually represents the values of the community; in the case of Martius, Menenius is the foil who speaks for the values of the community against the hero, whose "integrity" and "ideals" speak to the values of an individual (25–29). Mack also sees Shakespeare using a scene or passage after the climax or at the close of the tragedy that is at "cross purposes" with the tragic language, "detached" from the feelings of the hero (30). Although no example for *Coriolanus* is cited, the scene in which Martius bullies Aufidias's servants is followed by a long, amusing passage. The three servants comment on the great strength of Martius and Aufidias, which then leads them to a discussion of peace and war. Their domestic speech and jesting, Mack would say, is not "comic relief," but "the central dialogue of tragic experience" (30), the great individual in dialogue with the members of a community going about their everyday life.

Mack's claims about some of Shakespeare's patterns of construction are useful observations on Shakespeare's development as a tragic poet. Given the several traditions of "tragedy" that Shakespeare inherited, exploring Shakespeare's tragedies and the way that he mediates other tragic forms is eminently more constructive than pointing out Shakespeare's shortcomings in characterization. For some time, however, interpreting Shakespeare's tragic characters against specific tragic paradigms was popular with critics.

For example, Maurice Hunt in his examination of Martius shows how Martius is complemented in Aufidias, who "illuminates" (310) tragic traits not obvious in Martius. Thus, Aufidias becomes the character through whom Martius's tragic qualities are mediated. Hunt suggests that Aufidias and Martius, alter egos, in their "confederacy . . . become one with each other" (310). Subsequently, "each on occasion, loses his identity in the other" (310). Thus, Hunt can conclude that

> Aufidias acutely describes Coriolanus's *hamartia* as a tangled web of pride, flawed judgment, and a severe inflexibility of character (IV.vii.35–49). The *anagnorisis* of the tragic hero with which some confidence can be located in *Hamlet, Othello, King Lear,* and *Macbeth,* does not appear to occur within the least intellectual of Shakespeare's major tragic protagonists [Coriolanus]. Shakespeare gives Coriolanus only two short soliloquies, neither of which is particularly insightful. The salient feature of *Coriolanus* is, as Bradley noted, is the absence of it in "the exhibition of inward conflict, or the outburst of one or the other passion, terrible, heartrending, or glorious to witness." Instead, the playwight places the *anagnorisis* within Aufidias . . . at IV. iii. Aufidias's soliloquy is longer and more perceptive than either of Coriolanus's. It is as though one part of a single organism never communicates its insights to the other half, which dies for want of self-knowledge. (314)

Martius's not experiencing a particular kind of anagnorisis—recognition of a truth about himself—or not exhibiting other characteristics of tragic character favored by critics has possibly led to a lack of interest in studying Shakespeare's last tragic hero, whom at least one critic posits is the only tragic character of Shakespeare's who does not change.[5] Perhaps he is not seen to change, as Sailendra Kumar Sen suggests, because an "inner conflict . . . is not allowed to grow with the action" (344). Sen points to three conflicts that Martius faces, with each being resolved and Martius feeling he has resolved it to his satisfaction,[6] which in turn limits our perception of Martius as changing. Again, though, as Shakespeare appears to have developed his own kind of tragic character with elements from several tragic forms in evidence in each of the tragedies, analyzing the tragedies against a single paradigm will lead interpreters to draw conclusions that might not otherwise be considered.

As an example, not satisfied that *Coriolanus* is "tragic," some critics have found the play a satire. Oscar James Campbell suggests that contrary to presenting Martius as a tragic hero, Shakespeare shows him "partly as an object of scorn. Instead of ennobling Coriolanus through his fall and death, he mocks and ridicules him to the end. In brief, he fills the tragedy so full of the spirit of derision that the play can be understood only if it be recognized as perhaps the most successful of Shakespeare's satiric plays" (199). Another critic, James Holstun, suggests that Shakespeare "satirizes those generic aspects of tragedy that depend on an unquestioning faith in the complex medical and political analogy of the body politic, taking as his butt so many tragic conventions that it becomes difficult to think of *Coriolanus* as sharing a dramatic genre with *Richard II*, *Julius Caesar*, and *Hamlet*" (486). Karen Aubrey more fully develops the idea of the play being a satire, claiming that Shakespeare "uses the vehicle of tragedy both to mask the satire and to simultaneously intensify it once it is recognized" (300). The play, she notes, is a satire of current political practices and problems in England. As a parallel to Jacobean England, Martius's Rome is ruled by a patrician order at conflict with its plebeians over community economics. Martius adheres vehemently to an ideal Roman society that no longer exists, and which he exposes for its hypocrisy, one of the purposes of satire (300–301). Granted, it is easy to see elements of the satiric in the play, but once we figure in the historical character of Martius, Roman tragedies, and a political culture so very different from our own, Martius is more than a "dull actor" playing his part until the end. His story is that of the great man whose community was not big enough for him.

PSYCHOANALYTIC

Coriolanus's character has engaged psychoanalytic critics for several reasons: the influence Volumnia has over her son, the relationship between Coriolanus and Aufidias, and Coriolanus's single-mindedness dominate to such an extent that we wonder why Coriolanus responds to his environment, to people, in such rigidly drawn lines. To be sure, tragic heroes are mimetic figures, assigned particular traits or personalities by their authors; they are not real people. On the other hand, knowing the tragic character mimics to some degree familiar human characteristics, we can explore the represented psyche of characters, as long as we bear in mind that tragic heroes are constructed within the confines of genre; what makes them heroic are character traits or personalities or spirits that defy norms. The ahistorical nature of some psychoanalytic criticism has erred in not considering cultural milieu, such as Emmett Wilson's "Coriolanus: The Anxious Bridegroom." On the other hand, psychoanalytic readings do illuminate imagery or metaphors that might otherwise go untreated. And besides, psychoanalytic criticism is provocative.

In "The Anxious Bridegroom," Wilson does not mince words: the play is "an intensive exploration of a pathological mother-son relationship" (93). Volumnia is a dominant force in Martius's life, a widow who indoctrinates her son on Roman *virtus*. Superficially, it appears Martius is an obedient son, bringing glory and honor to his family, to his mother mostly, who more or less demands it. At an unconscious level, however,

Wilson says that anxieties about castration and the phallic mother are symbolized in Martius's attack on Corioles. His entry through the gates of the city, alone, followed by his emergence, a blood-covered victor, is symbolic of the defloration scene (97–98). Wilson explains that

> In the unconscious, defloration is equated with the castration of the sexual partner, and there is an associated dread of a mutilating retaliation. The feared punishment, castration, is symbolized in the battle by the danger of becoming entrapped within the gates, to be cut up and devoured. In the memory of defloration which follows the battle scenes, Coriolanus may well be attempting to deal with his terrifying discovery that he had created a sexual difference in his bride, by making her into a woman, i.e., a person who had been deprived of the phallus. Ultimately, the punishment that is dreaded for this act is a revenge by his mother on her son for having entertained these notions of assault against her body and, of course, on a deeper level, the woman who is castrated in the sexual act would be the phallic mother, Volumnia. (98)

This central and important moment in Martius's life, one that singles him out in Roman annals, seen from a psychoanalytical perspective, attempts to make sense of what appears to be an unusual mother-son relationship, and how it affects Martius's relationship with others. When he is banished, for instance, he seems to accept the punishment in better humor inside Rome's walls than outside. Once he has separated himself from Rome and his mother, he changes: he wants revenge, and for him, that means destroying Rome. An explanation in the text is not necessarily forthcoming, besides revenge, that is. According to Wilson, destroying Rome is the equivalent of destroying the phallic mother (109), for Martius fears being "engulfed by Volumnia in her ambitious designs to use him for her own goals. He is to function as her penile projection, by winning victories which will make her proud" (108). Historical and cultural considerations of the matron in republican Rome aside, Wilson's reading is of interest in that it illuminates the destructiveness of Roman *virtus* when taken to its extreme, as Volumnia does.

Volumnia may be ambitious for her son, but perhaps she has a reason. Bernard Paris suggests that Volumnia's status as a woman prevents her from engaging in the activities that Romans felt brought honor to one's name. Thus, she lives vicariously through her son, urging him to fight, win, and if he must, die, as "the glory he can achieve is more important to her than his company, his safety, or his life" (167). The "messages"

Coriolanus receives from his mother, Paris claims, influence his development (167), leading him to believe that if he fails to live up to his mother's expectation of him as a great Roman warrior of epic proportions, then he will lose her approval, upon which he thrives (168–69). Marilyn French, on the other hand, sees Martius seeking glory and honor for himself and no one else (270). In fact, she suggests that Coriolanus "articulates scorn for 'feminine' values implicit in Roman culture" (274), abhorring all that is feminine as being antithetical to manhood (274). Petitioning the people in the marketplace, he sees himself as feminine (274). The masculine principle, says French, dominates Martius. His need for control over nature, over need, desire, and so on, leads to "inhumaneness" (275), as French thinks Shakespeare shows in this play.

Martius's loss of a father, too, might be key to understanding Martius. Stanley Cavell's suggestion that Coriolanus's recollection of a man who had been kind to him in Corioles might be considered an "image of his father" (11) is provocative. Coriolanus's love for battle may be a way that he escapes the mother, thinks Cavell (11). In Aufidias, as Maurice Hunt shows, Martius finds not merely an alter ego; "the transformation of separate complementary individuals into a symbolic fusion of selves reveals dimensions of Coriolanus's character unilluminated by established analyses of the warriors as distinct alter egos" (310).

POLITICAL AND CULTURAL CRITICISM

During the 1980s, political criticism of Shakespeare's texts in the United States and Great Britain began to take shape with feminists and new historicists in the former, and Marxist criticism in the latter.[7] A play that pits patrician against plebeian undoubtedly would invite criticism from those concerned with class conflict, and indeed it has, although it should be noted that critics interested in parallels between the tragic hero and figures in early modern society contributed ideas long before Stephen Greenblatt renewed our interest in Shakespeare's historical milieu.[8] Paul Jorgenson suggests, for instance, that Martius appears more the adventurer soldier of early modern England, such as the Earl of Essex, than a Roman general. Essex, Jorgenson says, was a great fighter, like Martius, but not a good general (221–22). In fact, the early modern English, thinks Jorgenson, were less interested in warrior culture, in soldiers who were not of the gentleman order, as was Philip Sidney (225). Audiences would have seen not a Roman patrician-plebeian conflict, but rather a soldier at odds with an "uncongenial society" (235). Marxist critics, too, found of interest in the play Shakespeare's plebeians being represented as a "positive force" (106). As A. A. Smirnov writes, the play "reflects Shakespeare's profound disillusionment with absolutism, the courts, the state officials, and the upper classes, as is evidenced by the total absence of positive characters drawn from the privileged classes" (106). Although Smirnov finds Shakespeare bothered by the "political immaturity" of the people, he still believes Shakespeare had developed a "class consciousness of the English masses" (107), a position supported by some recent cultural critics.

Historicist and Marxist interpretations forward a critical position that acknowledges the role of literature in a culture's political ideology. Important, too, is the historical context of a play. Challenged are older critical approaches that saw Jacobean tragedy as representing ideals of order or harmony as seen in E.M.W. Tillyard's *The Elizabethan World Picture*. In *Radical Tragedy*, Jonathan Dollimore shows how Jacobean tragedy "discloses ideology as misrepresentation; it interrogates ideology from within, seizing on and exposing its contradictions and inconsistencies and offering alternative ways of understanding social and political process" (8). Of Martius, Dollimore says, "though identified in terms of an innate superiority he is in fact the ideological effect of powers antecedent to and independent of him" (218), which is true, as we know that Martius was nourished on the ideal of Roman *virtus* by his mother; moreover, Martius acknowledges himself as a servant to the state. He is what he is as long as he has what is valued by Rome.

New historicist critics have considered the ways that power and politics within a culture may be disseminated through literature. In her interest in showing cultural topicality in *Coriolanus*, Shannon Miller points out the several comparisons between James I and Coriolanus, primarily in personal manner and perspective on monarchical rule. James I, unlike Elizabeth I, would not mingle with the commoners nor cared to put on theatrical displays of his power (292). In the patrician Martius, like the aristocratic James, we see his contempt of mingling with the plebeians. (On the other hand, one must admit that he does interact with the plebeians frequently, spending a good deal of the play's time in their midst). James I's belief in divine right or his difficult relationship with Parliament may or may not be addressed in the characterization of Martius, but the idea is provocative, especially when what is considered at stake in the struggle is the power between the king and Parliament. Leah Marcus thinks that there are enough references in *Coriolanus* to "a language of civic 'liberties and franchises' . . . which carries strong topical reverberations with the jurisdictional battles in Shakespeare's London" (188). One example is concessions that James I made to London in a new charter in 1608. Finding that he needed money, James I was willing to grant London franchises and liberties they had not received previously (193). One such grant was that local authority could make arrests without interference by royal marshals, who would sometimes overrule them. Similarly, in *Coriolanus*, the senate has had to make concessions to the plebeians. Ultimately, Marcus will conclude that the play is not "impartial" in its politics, for she sees the play as a "tragedy for the aristocrat, and a victory for the citizen" (194).

Where Shakespeare's sympathies lie, with the plebeians or patricians, to be sure, is unknowable, but the play opens itself to interpretations that recognize the citizenry had a voice, which in Shakespeare's time is a progressive political perspective. For instance, Bryan Reynolds makes the case that the silence of the mutinous citizens in Act One, Scene One after the entrance of Coriolanus, who insults them, does not necessarily indicate "defeat or concession" on their part. Their silence might be perceived as a protest rather, as "[t]hey mock him with their silence—by ignoring his authority" (115). Moreover, when Coriolanus tells them to leave, they do not, again undermining any authority invested in his warrior or patrician status (115). These actions may go unnoticed to us who have been reared on ideas of freedom of speech, but they are significant in light of a cultural moment.

However we interpret voice or absence of voice, the voice of the plebeians is central to interpreting the social disorder, in this case class conflict, that imposes itself upon Coriolanus the warrior-soldier and upon the audience. Shakespeare's tragedies often open with scenes of social or civil unrest or disturbance. The audience is introduced immediately to the instability in the community in which the hero's or heroine's tragedy manifests itself. *Romeo and Juliet* opens with the servants of the Capulet and Montague households brawling; *Othello* opens with Iago urging Roderigo to discussion of a conspiracy. Even *Titus* shows the problems that arise when right to succession produces the worst leader. In *Coriolanus* the plebeians, or the nonpatricians, the equivalent of the aristocratic class in Shakespeare's time, explicitly state the cause of disorder in Rome: they explicitly identify Coriolanus as enemy to the people.

A political reading of the text illuminates the politics of the play in ways that popular beliefs about Shakespeare's attitude to the plebeians do not. Michael Bristol's reading of the class conflict in the play from Jürgen Habermas's notion of "legitimation crisis" is an excellent example.

Bristol defines *legitimation crisis* as that which affects a society in conflict over issues of authority and ultimately the authority's relationship to social organization, its economy and political practices (208). In turn, metaphors of opposition are generated, those "images of the good life" that assist in justifying authority or the power relations at hand. Bristol claims that what is significant about the Coriolanus story is that the plebeian is an "anonymous, collective player in the drama of political struggle [who] represents not only a full and coherent alternative political culture, but also the will to power of that political culture" (208). The plebeians figure in opposition to Coriolanus, whose appeal to authority rests in his charismatic authority, his "quasimagical capacity for violence rather than on any prophetic or persuasive gifts" (208). As Bristol points out, a charismatic authority destabilizes a social organization, but in this case, Coriolanus is accepted by the patricians, the current authority; it is the tribunes who challenge Coriolanus's right to authority (209). And, as we have seen, it is the tribunes whom Coriolanus despises, not the people. Although the tribunes' position in the current social organization is tenuous and dependent on their ability to stir unrest in the plebeians, their position is legitimated by the senate, just as Coriolanus's is. Yet the two sides antagonize each other, and they have differing views of social hierarchy: Coriolanus values war and a "command structure" that interferes with a "dispersed communal authority," says Bristol. Referencing Durkheim, Bristol points out that

> Rigid insistence on a vertical chain of command creates a situation where [*sic*] the only thing that matters is who's on top. Common people, normally organized in corporate bodies, sink into the condition of rabble as the result of material deprivation and of cultural violence. (210)

Referencing Styan, Bristol then suggests that

> Plebeian culture has resources that enable it to resist such a process of internal colonization and the suppression of their own diffuse authority by the figure of the great personality or *Führer*. The self-exclusion of the great public figure from the body of the people evokes "choric recrimination." (210)

Coriolanus is a personality, a charismatic figure, by virtue of brute strength, valor, courage, and a stubborn fidelity to a Roman ideal, but he is not a team player, desiring to bring glory home to his mother, to his family's name, as he has been taught. From the play's start, not only do we see the plebeians frustrated, we also see Coriolanus squabbling with them over their right to a voice, and it is eventually that voice that banishes him. The choric recrimination effectively manages to relieve the community of a destabilizing force, and presumably a restoration of order is afforded. A political reading like Bristol's thus shows how closely aligned, rather than how separate, are the political theme and the tragic characterization of Coriolanus.

Other considerations of the political theme include Phyllis Rackin's, which states that *Coriolanus* is Shakespeare demonstrating a form of "bad government" (137), a republic that lacked a mutual understanding between those who ruled and the ruled. Martius would be a failure as a political leader, nor could he be led. Martius's failure as a leader might be rooted, however, in a disconnection between the hero and his own aristocratic ideals. As Arthur Riss points out, Martius's desire to "o'erleap" the custom of petitioning the plebeians for their voice might have resulted from Martius's desire to maintain control of his body. Martius "falls because he asserts himself as a privately absolutely enclosed, literal 'body' in a society that mandates that he embrace an ideology of the body politic" (Riss 54).[9]

Although the analogy may have worn thin with subjects, Alex Garganigo argues compellingly that the organic metaphor of the body politic, quite popular with King James I, was made

> the centerpiece of his argument for Union. He insisted that his body natural, his physical body, had affected a union of the crowns of England and Scotland, that Union was "an Action, which God by the lawes of Nature . . . hath now in effect perfected in my Person," and that Parliament ought to make this union more systematic and permanent by uniting their legal and political systems. In effect, he wanted to codify body politic theory in law. (336)

Garganigo questions how the topicality of Jacobean political discourses about the body politic are or are not realized in *Coriolanus*, and determines, finally, that perhaps Shakespeare invokes the metaphor to criticize it and the "body-centered thinking" to which James clings (351), an observation that may help explain why the metaphor draws so much attention as being a failure.

FEMINIST

In *Shakespeare's Division of Experience*, Marilyn French considered the way that feminine and masculine "principles" operated in Shakespeare's plays. She described the masculine principle as "linear, temporal, and transcendent, for it aims to construct something in the world and within time that will enable the individual to transcend nature (which is cyclic), time, and mortality. The thing erected is a sort of immortality" (22). The masculine principle in Martius is what causes him to respond to any "taunt" against his "honor" (269). Honor is what Martius most cares about, believes French, so a taunt must be answered. Because he cares not about anyone but himself, he is antisocial, suggests French, and in being so, cares not what others think (270). He believes himself a god, and as such, transcends nature (270). The problem with Martius is that his masculine principle dominates too much, abhorring the feminine, and wanting too much control over nature (associated with the feminine principle) (275). French finds that the values imbued in the Roman concept of manliness were ultimately destructive, which is revealed in destructive Martius (276).

Janet Adleman in *Suffocating Mothers: Fantasies of Maternal Origin in Shakespeare's Plays, Hamlet to The Tempest* finds Coriolanus a character whose actions are dominated by a need to "ward off vulnerability to the mother" (130), in this case, to a nonnurturing mother. Coriolanus's "exaggerated masculinity" is a response to a fear of being exposed as weak and needy, possibly the result of being disengaged from dependence on his mother at too young an age. Suggesting that the need for food is what keeps humans "dependent on the world," Adelman shows how this play that begins with hungry, armed citizens who want corn released to them at fair prices contextualizes humans' vulnerability to hunger, human dependence upon the mother. Coriolanus's mother, Volumnia, Adelman points out, has early discouraged her son from dependence on food, and in turn has shown him the way to "feed on anger," being "only fed valiantness by her" (3.2.129) (148). Coriolanus has learned to reject food as a means to controlling his vulnerability or his dependence on nourishment, and by extension, his dependence on his mother. As Adelman puts it, "[t]he rigid masculinity that Coriolanus finds in war becomes a defense against acknowledgment of his neediness; he nearly succeeds in transforming himself from a vulnerable human creature into a grotesquely invulnerable and isolated thing" (149). The hungry mob, therefore, represents for Coriolanus vulnerability and neediness, dependence on another, the state, that he finds abhorrent (153–55). His banishment allows him the opportunity to seek out Aufidius, in whom he finds an ideal of warriorhood.

Martius's disengagement from maternal nurturing may not have succeeded in making him entirely independent of his mother, however. As Coppélia Kahn writes in *Roman Shakespeare: Warriors, Wounds, and Women*, women in Rome were respected in their maternal roles, and in the case of Volumnia, bearing a male, Volumnia "seized such access to the political sphere as Rome offered her" (148). Her access is dependent on her son, whom she claims in the play has gotten his "mould" and "frame" from her (148). His valiantness, Volumnia claims, came from her. She developed in him the *virtus* he valued. But as a patrician mother, she shares with a patrician father an exception to the practice of kneeling to men: Volumnia would never have to kneel to Coriolanus, but when she petitions him not to destroy Rome, she kneels. Kahn writes:

> Because of the way that she framed [Martius] to *virtus*, Coriolanus owes more than his physical existence to his mother. In kneeling to her son she reverses the usual gesture of indebtedness only to evoke more pointedly the unusual totality of his debt to her so that he will capitulate to her. (157)

In Martius's Rome, it appears, the man who lives the ideal of *virtus* is a man never free from duty to state or family, or the psychological and emotional ties that bind him. This, it seems, is the general idea, Shakespeare wanted to express.

NOTES

1. See Chapters 4 and 6.
2. D.F. Bratchell, ed., *Shakespearean Tragedy* (New York: Routledge, 1960), p. 31.
3. Ibid., p. 36, says that Dryden thought that Shakespeare wasted "opportunities" to "instruct and delight" and that he "reject[ed] those exhibitions which would be more affecting for the sake of those which are more easy." We see in Nahum Tate's adaptation of *Coriolanus*, *The Ingratitude of the Commonwealth* (1688/1689), the dramatist's urge to clarify purpose, to make sure that the lesson is clear and not open for interpretation. As we shall see in the next section, the modifications were not improvements on Shakespeare's works, but their being interpreted by dramatists is important to the critical tradition of *Coriolanus*. Not only was the text interpreted to suit the tastes of an age's dramatists and theatergoers, but it was also edited as a text in need of "repair."

4. In 1904, Bradley's lectures on Shakespearean tragedy were published. In those, Bradley narrowed his focus to the four characters who he felt most represented Shakespeare's conception of tragic character (as Bradley perceived it). A. C. Bradley, "Coriolanus," *The Annual Shakespeare Lectures* (1912).

5. Norman Rabkin, "Coriolanus: The Tragedy of Politics," *Shakespeare Quarterly* 17 (1966), says in "no other tragedy of Shakespeare is there so little growth or change in character" (211). In tragedy, critics look at conventions common to tragedies, such as a hero's showing an understanding of self and thus exhibiting a level of psychological or emotional growth as a human being. It is easy to see why critics would find this true of Martius: at his death, he appears to be fighting the same anxieties that dominate his character throughout the play, his fear of not being perceived as a man. On the other hand, his recognition that he is no more than a mortal subject to the laws of nature in Act Five is quite moving, and for Martius, hard-learned.

6. Sailendra Kumar Sen, "What Happens in *Coriolanus*," *Shakespeare Quarterly* 9 (1958), p. 337, cites the following scenes: "(1) at the time of election: 2.2.140–155 and 2.3.53–157; (2) on the question of conciliating the people: 3.2.99–145 and 3.3.38–61; (3) the deputations of Cominius 5.1.64–70, Menenius 5.3.8–16, and Volumnia 5.3.22–189."

7. Walter Cohen, "Political Criticism of Shakespeare," in *Shakespeare Reproduced: The Text in History & Ideology*, ed. Jean E. Howard and Marion F. O'Connor (New York: Routledge, 1990), p. 19.

8. See Stephen Greenblatt's *Renaissance Self-Fashioning: From More to Shakespeare* (Chicago: U of Chicago P, 1980) for essays on the Renaissance from a "new historicist" point of view.

9. Paul Cefalu, " 'The End of Absolutism': Shakespeare's *Coriolanus* and the Consensual Nature of the Early Modern State," *Renaissance Forum* 4 (2000), par. 7, says, however, that James's government was not as absolutist as presumed by critics such as Riss, which challenges Riss's "possessive individualist reading."

6

THE PLAY IN PERFORMANCE

Whether or not *Coriolanus* was performed during Shakespeare's lifetime is not known with certainty,[1] but records show that it was staged in the Restoration, a period whose dramatists and critics promoted a vision of poetic representation on stage and in writing unlike that of their talented literary predecessors. Although Shakespeare's plays were revived during the period, adaptations and interpolated versions dominated the stage, presumably to suit the tastes of the period. England had matured as a nation by 1660, having executed a king and experienced a commonwealth under Oliver Cromwell during the interregnum. Charles II sat on the English throne, but his England was not the same England as that of his father, Charles I. Charles I's beheading signified an end to the absolutist ideal of kingship which James I of Shakespeare's England so adamantly maintained was his due. With the concept of divine right to rule seriously challenged by the English people upon Charles I's execution, other concepts of human and divine rights necessarily would develop. Naturally, the idea of a tragic hero was bound to be affected by the evolving concepts of humans and their social order. Thus, when Coriolanus makes his debut on the Restoration stage, the hero who emerges has lost much of the superhuman energy and the divine captured by Shakespeare. He is a more domestic creature, a citizen of the state, a god-fearing husband.[2]

Shakespeare's *Coriolanus* became the property of Thomas Killigrew's King's Company 1668/1669, one of the two companies licensed to operate under Charles II. Nahum Tate then adapted it in a play entitled *The Ingratitude of a Commonwealth, or The Fall of Caius Martius Coriolanus*, which was possibly performed sometime during December 1681 through

January 1682.[3] Considered anti-Whig propaganda, Tate's *Ingratitude* at the outset stated its political intent. In the letter to his patron, Lord Herbert, which prefaces the play, Tate wrote of his indebtedness to Shakespeare's play that his patron would find that "Upon a close view of this Story there appear'd in some Passages, no small Resemblance with the busie Faction of our own time" so "What offence [is there] to any good Subject in Stygmatizing on the Stage, those Troublers of the State, that out of private Interest or Mallice, Seduce the Multitude to Ingratitude, against Persons that are not only plac't in Rightful Power above them; but also the Heroes and Defender of their Country."[4] Tate goes on to argue that examples of what happens when a commonwealth has a "blind Compliance with their popular Misleaders" are of no "harm."[5] Thus, Shakespeare's *Coriolanus* becomes for Tate a play that can be used to make a political statement and showcase other popular conventions of the period, mostly those that come with having women perform women's parts.

The *Ingratitude*, probably based upon the third folio edition of Shakespeare's works, utilizes much of *Coriolanus*'s plot, theme, and language, but it modifies the play to accommodate the staging practices of the time, so we find the play's women performing parts in ways similar to other dramas of the period.[6] Valeria's role, minute in Shakespeare's play, is expanded in Tate's. A figure common in the comedy of manners was the young, self-absorbed, superficial woman who is presented as a satire of the nonproductiveness of the leisure class. Some of the play's most serious moments are interrupted by the entrance of Valeria, "An affected, talkative, fantastical lady,"[7] who probably provides the audience a visual treat in her costume, if not providing a woman actor a part in a play.[8] Then again, she may perform a useful function in the characterization of Coriolanus: a satiric mirror to some of his personality flaws.

In one scene, Volumnia and Virgilia are discussing Coriolanus's ability to battle Aufidius, when Valeria is announced as a visitor. Giving no one else a chance to speak, Valeria asserts that if anything happens in battle, she will be the first to know, as her many soldier/suitors send her news daily of the battle. Valeria's letters from suitors are so many that she must burn them, she tells Volumnia and Virgilia.[9] In effect, Valeria burns the news to which she claims to be privy, making her assertion about having knowledge of the battle worthless. Valeria would have drawn laughs for meeting audience expectations of superciliousness; Virgilia, in contrast, is the sober Roman matron, but given her noble lines in the play, there is little to suggest she needed a contrast to emphasize her worth. Valeria interrupts another important scene when she appears to Volumnia, in great haste, she claims, but with enough time for a digression; she complains about the men of the day, their lack of "thought . . . science . . . Eloquence . . . breeding" (3.2.10), complains about another Roman lady, Galatea, who is an "Eternal Talker!" and goes on to explain how she herself plays contrary with men, "to seem Merry when [she is] sad; Sad when [she is] Merry" (3.2.55). She finally exits with her pages to be followed on stage by Coriolanus, Menenius, and other nobles; here Volumnia, who has said little in response to the inane chatter of Valeria, chides her son for his tactless and impolitic manner in the senate as he argues with the tribunes over the consulship. The silly diversion that anticipates the play's climax is not entirely without purpose, however: Valeria's description of the Lady Galatea's speech might have been a description of Coriolanus's to the tribunes and citizens: "Her Tongue's the perpetual Motion, and she affects such hard Words, such an obdurate Phrase, that she exposes her self a publick Ludibry to the Universe" (3.2.23–25).

The audience might laugh at Valeria's description of her own self, but at another level, they must be aware that Coriolanus's tongue is uncontrollable and hard on the hearers for whom he has contempt. Tate attempts to remove some of the offensiveness of Shakespeare's Coriolanus, and thereby the offensiveness that might be associated with the patrician (Tory) class. Thus, Valeria's lighthearted intrusion might be perceived as mitigating, as is Coriolanus's assuring his mother he will return to the senate and guard his tongue after she chides him for his "absolute" manner and urges him to buy peace with a "feign'd Compliance" (3.2.74) to the tribunes and citizens, especially if his doing otherwise will threaten the lives of friends and family. Volumnia's speech to her son recognizes the power invested in the speech act to control our environments and those who surround us. Valeria's empty chatter, which reveals the vacancy of her mind and heart, is nonthreatening. Coriolanus's brutal and heartfelt disgust with a citizenry so vacant of values, honor, and ideas, at least from his perspective, is threatening.

Valeria bursts in on Act Five, when Virgilia, Volumnia, and young Martius are being hailed by the Roman citizens for their success in urging Coriolanus not to attack Rome. Desiring to ride the coattails of the successful party, Valeria makes excuses for not traveling with them to petition Coriolanus and attempting to secure peace from the "dearest Obstinate man; Which I confess in a Vulgar Person, were not inordinately, unsufferable; but in him it looks so Grand, Heroick, and August, that no Aera Catalogue, Chronicle, Register, or Annals of Time can ever" (5.17–19). Here Valeria drops off, seeing young Martius, which causes her to lose her train of thought. She leaves off her hyperbole to chatter about young Martius. Valeria speaks of Coriolanus as if he were one of her many suitors, completely nullifying his heroic stature, as if her reference to his chronicled heroics were not diminishing enough.

Perhaps Tate wanted to make Coriolanus more manlike than godlike, more sensitive than arrogant. For instance, Coriolanus offers to find out the name of the old man in *Ingratitude*, whereas in Shakespeare's text, Coriolanus cannot even remember his name; moreover, being thirsty, Coriolanus calls for wine, forgetting the old man entirely. In *Ingratitude*, Coriolanus says, "Now let us sacrifice to the Gods, and pray / For many Rival Days, to This on Rome; / Then Yield our Pious Rites, to our Slain Friends" (1.4.70–72). Tate's Coriolanus recognizes his fellowship with other humans and prioritizes it, whereas Shakespeare's Coriolanus prioritizes his physical needs: he is tired and thirsty from battle. Tate's Tory Coriolanus puts the gods and then others first.

With the advent of women on stage came another theme that Tate exploited: rape scenes. Tate included in his adaptation a theme not treated in Shakespeare's play: Aufidias's desire for Virgilia. Tate has Aufidias seeking revenge on Coriolanus, not for honor or glory, but because Coriolanus robbed him of his love interest, Virgilia. In front of the dying Coriolanus, Aufidias threatens to rape Virgilia.[10] The rape does not occur, however, as Aufidias finds that he cannot go through with his revenge. Coriolanus is shown the dying, loving husband, with his wife by his side, not the great godlike hero cut down by Aufidias's hired-hands, alone. As Shakespeare had Coriolanus enter the city of Corioles alone and defeat the Volscians, he has him die alone at the hands of the Volscians, no fellow Romans to succor him.

Thus, *Coriolanus*'s first showing, it seems, offered up a god-fearing, domestic, repentant citizen-hero, hardly the solitary, superhuman enigma that is Shakespeare's troubled hero. Thomas G. Olsen summarizes Tate's effort as a "retreat into the sentimentality of prevailing dramatic conventions" which "announce[d] the problems inherent in grafting scions onto Shakespeare's stock and rearranging the jewels (or rubble) of his plays to suit prevailing political needs" (422). Tate's doing so is what makes *The Ingratitude* important in theater history: he begins a pattern of exploiting Shakespeare's *Coriolanus* for political ends but also, and I think perhaps more important, of modifying Shakespeare's text to suit any number of seeming theatrical problems or tastes.

When *Coriolanus* next appeared on the English stage, it was Shakespeare's, at Lincoln's Inn Fields in December of 1718, although it may have been staged at the same theater in 1699.[11] Not much is known about either production, as the references to either, such as the *Daily Courant* of 1718, which advertises Shakespeare's *Coriolanus* and notes that it has not been played in twenty years, also informs readers that the play will have "Machines, Triumphal Arches, and other Decorations after the Custom of the Romans."[12]

The next known production of a Coriolanus play was John Dennis's adaptation, *The Invader of His Country: or The Fatal Resentment*, staged at Drury Lane November 11–13, 1719.[13] Dennis claims in the dedication to the Lord Chamberlain, Thomas, Duke of Newcastle, that his play is "the *Coriolanus* of *Shakespear* alter'd by [him]" (A2).[14] It is modified and like all adaptations of Shakespeare's last tragedy, not necessarily improved by the adapter's hand. Dennis claimed order needed to be imposed on Shakespeare's "*wild Confusion*" (Prologue).[15] Like Tate's play, its politics are stated upfront, although unlike Tate, Dennis is on the side of the people; it is the "*Storms of Factious Rage*" that Dennis opposes (Prologue). Referring to recent events in English history, Dennis writes in a lengthy address to his viewers,

> *For as when* Britain's *Rebel Sons of late*
> *Combin'd with Foreign Foes t'invade the State,*
> *She to your Valour and your Conduct owes,*
> *That she subdued and crush'd her num'rous Foes.* (Prologue)

Thus, the play becomes a celebration of British people who prevented the Old Pretender from breaching its border. The Old Pretender was James Edward Stuart, son of Louis XIV. At the death of James II in 1701, the French king recognized his son as rightful heir to the English throne. By 1708, James Edward Stuart gathered enough support from some in Scotland and England, and had raised a French army of 6,000. He landed at the Firth of Forth, but was defeated. Although *The Invader* was not staged until 1719, Dennis probably wrote it in 1708. In 1717 or 1718, Dennis asked the Drury Lane proprietors to stage the play; they agreed, which seemed fortuitous for Dennis, as James Edward Stuart had again found support for an invasion of England from Sweden and Spain in 1718. The play was delayed, however, and not performed until November 1719, when it ran three nights before it was closed.

Dennis used the dedication to complain that the Drury Lane proprietors were responsible for its early closing.[16] The fact is, the adaptation is not as great as Dennis claims. Whiggish in sympathy, the characterization of Coriolanus is stilted, there being a loss of tragic awe and magnanimity that marks Shakespeare's hero. Dennis's play is proscriptive, there being no mystery about the author's political views; Shakespeare's political sympathies are ambiguous. Following the cited passage above, Dennis writes:

> *We shew to Night, such Treasons to prevent,*
> *That their Guilt's follow'd by their Punishment,*
> *That Heav'n's the Guardian of our Rightful Cause*
> *And watches o'er our Sov'reign and our Laws.* (Prologue)

The play is informed by the providentialism seen in Shakespeare's history plays, with treasonous characters receiving their just due. Hints of Coriolanus's propensity toward treason appear early in the play, when he lets the audience know that he "hates the people." The play begins with the battle at Corioles underway. Dennis's Coriolanus saves the battle for Cominius, who will be honored with the win. Cominius feels that it is time that Coriolanus be advanced to a consul position, although he lets Coriolanus know that he has a "Blemish" that will ruin his chances for success:

> Thou hast a Soul too haughty and severe
> For one who lives in a Free State, a State
> That's so much founded on Equality.
> You have been too harsh, and have provok'd the People. (11)

To which Coriolanus responds: "I hate the People" (11).

Dennis's narrow-minded Coriolanus cannot see outside the small world that he has created for himself. Cominius tells Coriolanus that he is "ungrateful," yet Coriolanus continues to urge his position, saying that the people are "insolen[t]." When Cominius asks Coriolanus whether or not he fights for all Romans when he fights for Rome, Coriolanus claims that the Romans are the patricians and senate, and no one else. Cominius reminds him that all Romans are from the same stock, as Act One comes to a close, leaving the audience with an image of Coriolanus as a class chauvinist (11). Shakespeare's Coriolanus, on the other hand, does not hate the people,[17] although the tribunes claim that he does. Shakespeare's Sicinius tells the plebeians that Coriolanus feels an "inveterate hate" toward them (2.3.224), which Dennis translates as Coriolanus's feelings. These feelings of hate are shown as uncontrolled when Coriolanus stands before the people in the shirt of humility in Dennis's play. A citizen who has watched other citizens approach Coriolanus and be treated mockingly says,

> I have not stood by, and observed for nothing. He has flouted all my Companions, and I suppose I am to expect the like usage in my turn, which to prevent by *Hercules*, I'll try to mortify this haughty, doughty Heroe. (26)

The citizen approaches Coriolanus, pretending that he does not know why Coriolanus appears in the marketplace in humble clothing. As a Roman, the citizen knows well the tradition of candidates for consul standing before the people in a humble robe, and he knows the famous Roman soldier. Coriolanus asks the citizen if he knows why he is standing in the forum, and the citizen pretends ignorance; the citizen goes so far as to call Coriolanus a Volscian, which of course angers Coriolanus. Coriolanus begins to beat him, chasing him off the stage. This can, of course, be seen as humorous, that Dennis is working off of Shakespeare's opening to *Coriolanus*. Critic Norman Rabkin points out that Coriolanus's entry in Shakespeare's play, with his threats to reduce the population of Rome by slaying them, might be read satirically, and perhaps Dennis senses the theatrical potential for satire.[18] Yet, even if Coriolanus plays over-the-top, Coriolanus's display of rage and his beating of the citizen are a visual expression of his inability to repress his hostility toward the plebeians. Shakespeare's Coriolanus is naive about the plebeian class, to be sure, and is free with his tongue regarding what he perceives as their innate ignorance; taunted by the tribunes and banished by their underhanded manipulation of the plebeians, Shakespeare's Coriolanus loses control and directs his rage at the people's voices, "their stinking breaths," their ability to make judgments about him. All Romans, patricians and plebeians alike, earn his contempt. In the way that Coriolanus sees Rome as embodying an ideal that he feels he lives, Coriolanus finds himself at war with Rome, all of Rome, which has failed him. Dennis's Coriolanus fails to rise to that level of complexity, his purpose being to make the patrician class look and act callous toward the free people.

Although Dennis's adaptation retained much of Shakespeare's language and plot, his purpose was uncongenial to Shakespeare's tragic hero, reducing him to a lawless Jacobite, in the same way Tate reduced his Coriolanus to a domestic hero. As Shakespeare's *Coriolanus* begins with an uprising of the people, the play seems to have attracted the earliest Restoration dramatists because it addressed questions of class conflict—addressed, not answered. Shakespeare gave us more than a conflict, however; he gave us a hero whose severe approach to a perceived ideal of social order proved his undoing. His misguided view of Roman-ness, nurtured by his mother, simultaneously tapped his strengths and weaknesses. Devotion to state and family led him to aspire to military greatness. He lived by a code of conduct that was practiced more in the breach than not, which put him in a position of isolation. What he valued, great military courage and valor, was not valued by all; thus, he admires most Aufidias, enemy to Rome. No Roman strikes him as his match. His great feats are awe-inspiring and terrifying, winning him praise, honor, and glory, but they set him off as alien, different. He bears none of the ordinary vices: greed, lust, infidelity, or overindulgence. For all of his strength, he is fragile, and in some ways, too human. Character, not plot, unity, or politics, is the center of Shakespeare's *Coriolanus*.

When Dennis uses some of Shakespeare's hero's lines but not others, or when he paraphrases passages and lines, or cuts whole scenes, the result is confusion in purpose. Does he want to show the people as deserving a voice and Coriolanus as one who would prevent that? Coriolanus's speech on how appealing to the people for their voices requires him to be false to himself, a soldier used to leading men in war, seems a contradiction to the Coriolanus that Dennis has kicking servants in Aufidias's kitchen. He is a martial hero from Shakespeare one moment, a bully of Dennis's design in another. Then the tribunes, representatives of the people, are presented as singularly malevolent; they are even dragged off and presumably killed by the people, who are angry at their instigating Coriolanus's banishment. The people, too, appear inconstant, unable to think for themselves, easily misled. When the tribunes urge them to voice their vote to banish Coriolanus, they do so, even though he was welcomed back from Corioles by them; they want Coriolanus to protect them when they are threatened by the Volscians after the banishment. Dennis did not need to show them so gullible, nor representatives of the people as self-serving. In Act Two, Dennis has Brutus saying of their plan to prevent Coriolanus from gaining a consulship:

> And we the Rabble have wisely enrag'd,
> To be reveng'd of this *Coriolanus*;
> Whome we must ruine, or our selves be lost.
> This proud *Patrician* threats our new-born Pow'r,
> Which either yet we must retain, or die.

So much, we have enraged the haughty Senate,
By heading that Sedition of the People,
Which forc'd the Fathers to create us Tribunes;
And Tribunes we must be, or must be nothing. (30)

The real criminals in Dennis's text are the tribunes, who are "the people," as they were in Shakespeare's. They are responsible for social unrest in Rome, and the series of chaotic events that led to Coriolanus's banishment. These men undo the hero and the people, yet the plebeians ridding Rome of Coriolanus and the tribunes leave them with no defense or representation. Dennis's play thus creates as many problems as it seeks to answer.

The next time *Coriolanus* was staged, January 13, 1749, at Covent Garden, it was James Thomson's blank verse *Coriolanus*,[19] being performed after the death of Thomson half a year earlier.[20] Thomson used "the pattern established by Dionysius and Livy, rather than on the Plutarch-Shakespeare pattern used by Tate and Dennis."[21] Thomson's version begins with Coriolanus banished already. Rather than an adaptation of Shakespeare's, Thomson's play is his own, and interestingly, parts of his play were interpolated into later versions of "Shakespeare's" *Coriolanus*. The play focuses on Tullus Aufidias's desire to revenge Coriolanus's destruction of his city, Coriolanus's desire for revenge over his banishment, his mother's petition to save Rome, and Coriolanus's death. The play's language is elevated and heavily sprinkled with terms like "noble" and references to the gods. One critical difference between Thomson's text and prior dramatic treatments is having Veturia (Volumnia in Shakespeare) pulling out a knife and threatening to kill herself during her petition to Coriolanus. Failing to move Coriolanus with her arguments, Veturia, angry, threatens,

I came not hither
To be sent back rejected, baffled, sham'd,
Hateful to Rome, because I am thy mother:
A Roman matron knows, in such extremes,
What to take—and thus I came provided.
[Drawing from under her robe a dagger.]
Go, barbarous son! go! double parricide!
Rush o'er my corse to thy belov'd revenge!
Tread on the bleeding breast of her, to whom
Thou ow'st thy life!—Lo, thy first victim. (5.1.193–201)[22]

This theatrical gesture and Veturia's hyperbolic language no doubt were exciting drama. Veturia's threat to kill herself, too, puts Coriolanus in a no-win situation. In front of the Volscians, Veturia's suicide would be judged harshly by any group of men; if Veturia walks away alive, she has won her appeal, which will also be judged harshly by the enemy. Coriolanus's death is secured.

The play ran for ten performances, with some success, but was never shown on the London stage again in its original format.[23] Oddly, James Quin (1693–1766), at age fifty-six, was cast as Coriolanus, a man much too old to represent the more youthful son of Veturia, but probably a good fit for the blank-verse role because he employed what was considered an outmoded style of acting still favored by some tragedians.[24] Audiences enjoyed him, though, which may explain his playing Coriolanus, a part that would be played by some of the English stage's greatest actors in high tragic fashion. A sketch of Quin playing Coriolanus in a tonnelet, or hooped skirt worn by eighteenth-century tragedians, has been preserved, giving us a rare glimpse of a mid-eighteenth-century Coriolanus.[25]

In 1754, David Garrick (1717–1789), the respected English actor, manager, and dramatist, revived Shakespeare's *Coriolanus* for a performance at Drury Lane for an eight-day run on November 11.[26] Garrick's revival of Shakespeare marked the first time in thirty years that Shakespeare's play had been on the stage. With 1,000 lines cut, it was the edition that would appear in Bell's 1774 edition.[27] Shakespeare's text, Robert D. Hume reminds us, during the seventeenth and eighteenth centuries was a theatrical text, and for those in theater, Shakespeare's works were "regarded as theatrical vehicles subject to free appropriation, and this remained basically true long after claims started to be made for plays as works of literature" (48). Thus, theater promptbooks and published stage promptbooks look little like the literary editions that we read today or like those texts that are used by theater ensembles. What was deemed successful in the theater was retained when adaptations and revivals of Shakespeare were drafted.

Thomas Sheridan's adaptation, *Coriolanus, or the Roman Matron*, an "amalgam of Thomson and Shakespeare," was staged December 10, 1754.[28] It enjoyed a long run on the stage. Sheridan's *Coriolanus* is a more refined version of the virtuous Roman soldier than is Shakespeare's. What is great and noble about Coriolanus is constantly remarked upon by his patrician peers. The play does not open with Coriolanus arguing with the plebeians, but with Veturia, his mother, singing his praises. Scenes in which Coriolanus was wont to play the bully in Shakespeare's play are

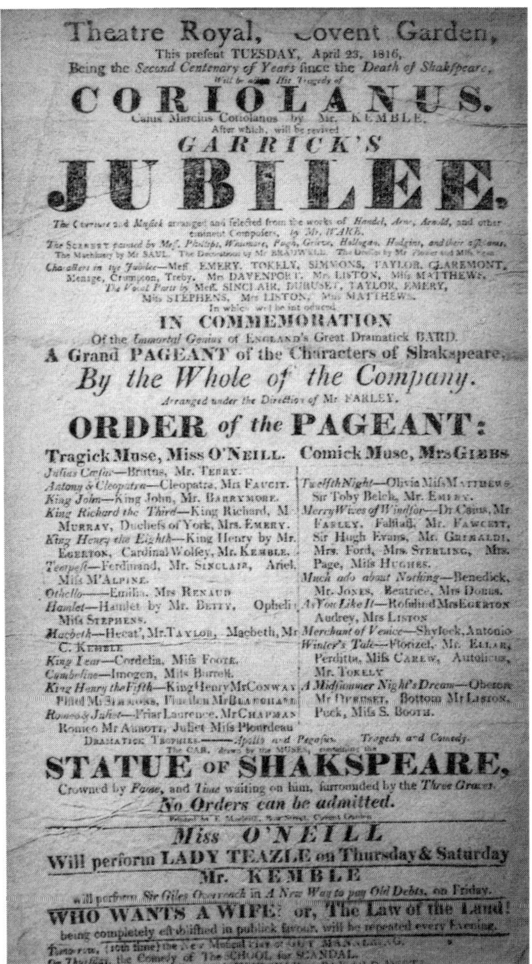

Playbill for a performance of *Coriolanus* at Theatre Royal, Covent Garden 1816. By Permission of the Shakespeare Birthplace Trust.

deleted, such as when he visits Tullus Aufidias's house. Act Three of *The Roman Matron* opens with Tullus and a Voluscius at a Volscian camp planning their next move against Rome. An officer appears to tell Tullus,

> My lord,
> One of exalted port, his visage hid,
> Has plac'd himself upon your sacred hearth

> Beneath the dread protection of your lares,
> And sits majestic there in solemn silence.[29]

Moreover, the officer claims that he felt that he was in the "presence of some god" (6). As we have seen so often in Shakespeare's play and adaptations of it, it is the patricians, senators, soldiers, and those who approve of Roman ideals of valor and warriorhood who make claims of nobility for Coriolanus. To keep that image intact, Sheridan omits Coriolanus's coming upon the three servants in Tullus's kitchen and patronizing them. Instead he appears a mysterious yet godlike figure. Still, the play is essentially Shakespeare's, with Shakespeare's spirited opponent to plebeian representation stripped to a hero-victim of plebeian vulgarity and tribunal corruption. Lacking is the persistence of Coriolanus's objections to plebeian representation, which are so singularly a part of Coriolanus's personality in Shakespeare's play. The plebeians and tribunes in Sheridan's version drive Coriolanus out of Rome, giving Coriolanus a motivation to turn against Rome. That the plebeians might have a just complaint or a right to a voice is not important. Clearly, for Sheridan, they are vulgar, unlike the noble patricians. The plebeians and tribunes banish Coriolanus, the patrician Veturia convinces him to not storm Rome. The patrician women recuperate the order to Rome that has been subverted by the tribunes and their abuse of power. Sheridan's was a theatrical spectacle, it must be remembered. One addition he made to the play was an "ovation," a procession in which Coriolanus is preceded and followed into Rome by priests, soldiers, family, and consuls after his victory at Corioles (Ripley 106). Even with this edition, Shakespeare's play text had been cut to the extent that the play only lasted one hour and forty-five minutes.[30]

A commercial enterprise, theaters, companies of actors, poets, and other involved in the theater business lived on the profits of playgoers. As we have seen with even the first adaptations of Shakespeare, plays were written and performed to suit audience tastes, as well as critical tastes. Playhouse practices and traditions, too, were key to a play's execution on stage. Eventually, though, Shakespeare's text would emerge on stage as Shakespeare's, a text designed for the stage, to be sure.

According to Ralph Berry, it was John Philip Kemble's (1757–1823) *Coriolanus*, first played at Drury Lane in 1789, that "demand[ed] to be taken seriously, as a capable, sustained, and celebrated attempt to expound the play to a contemporary audience" ("Metamorphoses," 173). Shakespeare was "restored" in much of Kemble's version, but Kemble "kept some of Sheridan's cuts, some of Thomson, and also some of Sheridan's additions."[31] Kemble apparently captured and presented to audiences a characterization of Coriolanus that emphasized some of the Roman patrician's "rigidity" of mind. Berry thinks that period pictures reveal Kemble's idea of Coriolanus as "stern, forbidding, and dyspeptic," the focus entirely on the hero, not on the politics of the play ("Metamorphoses," 174).

A contemporary critic on one of the numerous plays in which Kemble performed this part, William Hazlitt, observed that Kemble excelled "in the development of some one sentiment or exclusive passion" which Hazlitt says Kemble does by maintaining the "same haughty dignity of demeanor, the same energy of will, and unbending sternness of will throughout."[32] Not only did Kemble impress audiences with his characterization, but in his 1811 performance at Covent Garden, which he managed, set design and costumes were visually exciting and apparently worth the expense.[33]

George Odell believes that "Coriolanus has come down in theatrical history as that part in Shakespeare which most exactly fitted the style and personality of John Kemble" (2:104) even if his first performance in 1789 was not the most memorable.[34] In effect, Kemble is Coriolanus as later Coriolanus-actors would presume, with one exception: Edmund Kean (1789–1833). Kean's acting style created a "paradigm shift" in the presentation of Shakespearean character. He introduced a "mode of acting emphasizing intense emotions and marked mood swings [that] won out over the neo-classical restrained style of the Kembles, who had seemed to emphasize showing ideals in statuesque standard poses ('points' held for applause) rather than embodying the emotional explosiveness of human experiences in made-to-order fluid combinations."[35] His style drew mixed responses, so Tracy Davis tell us: "Kean was popular with the working classes and the social melting pot of the [theater] pit, yet was frequently dismissed as an overrated gesticulator by precisely that sector of Tories who frequented the [theater's] front boxes" (936). Whatever the case, his acting style apparently was not suited to the role of Coriolanus.

Kean played the great patrician Coriolanus January 24 or 25, 1820, to his fans, although the play did not come off as well as hoped. The short run, compared to the many times the other great actors and actor-managers of the period played Coriolanus, is telling. Kean was one of the most successful actors of his time, yet could not manage a convincing Coriolanus. Thus, the nineteenth-century Coriolanus-actor who was most successful, it appears, was the one who followed the Kemble formula.

Usually the successful actor was distinguished by not only being able to present classical-styled Coriolanuses, but also being able to make genial changes that audiences or actors enjoyed. Actor-manager William Charles Macready (1793–1873) was the first to exploit the Roman populace, casting many for the part.[36] One period writer describes the stage full: men with staves, pickaxes, and other implements, donned in apparel that might suggest free men, not serfs, against the aristocracy.[37] The crowd or people become a significant part of the play at this point, actually being called a protagonist in a later performance by Sir Frank Robert Benson (1858–1939).[38] Despite modeling his acting of the part on Kemble, Macready was not quite as popular, even if the spectacles were well-regarded. One reason may be the lukewarm feeling that he had toward the play. In an entry in his diary on December 19, 1833, Macready notes that he "[r]ead through *Coriolanus*, which I am very anxious to make a part of, but fear the uninteresting nature of the story and the recollection of Kemble are objections too strong to be overcome" (86). Still, he passed on the Kemble tradition to later actors. Macready played Coriolanus in famed venues, first performing the role at Covent Garden in 1819, and then last performing it at Covent in 1938, a year he played the role at least nine times at the Garden.

Another player during the period also represented Coriolanus on the stage, John Vandenhoff (1790–1861). He took Coriolanus to more theaters outside London than other actors of his time and played the role for over thirty years. Beginning in 1820, when he opened at the Theatre Royal in Liverpool, Vandenhoff primarily played "Theatre Royal" stages in Edinburgh, Manchester, Haymarket, Dublin, Carlisle, and Birmingham. In 1837, he took Coriolanus to America, where he played the Chestnut Street Theater in Philadelphia and the National and Park theaters in New York, Alabama, and Boston, keeping the Coriolanus tradition alive for Scots, Americans, and Irish through the mid-nineteenth century.

Samuel Phelps (1804–1878), who had played Aufidias under Vandenhoff's Coriolanus, finally had the opportunity to play the Roman hero. From 1848 through 1860 Phelps played Coriolanus on about thirty occasions at Sadler's Wells. Like his predecessors, Phelps focused on presenting a noble and virtuous Coriolanus in lavish settings. As the theater evolved, the visual aesthetics became more prominent features of the theatrical entertainments. According to Ripley, Phelps also borrowed the imperial setting of Rome from Kemble, not the early, primitive period in which it is set, and he also added Macready's use of "Etruscan mise-en-scene for the Volscian episodes, the first recorded attempt to distinguish visually between Roman and Volscian cultures" (177).

The play was ignored in England until Sir Frank Benson brought it to the stage in 1893, and then Benson appears to have followed much of Phelps's stage play.[39] For about thirty years, says Ripley, Benson gave his audiences a "beau ideal" of Coriolanus (198), believing it necessary to preserve the classicism of the character against the encroaching "realist" style (199). Benson also relieved the play of the lavish setting, preferring to focus on the characters and their voices (199).

Sir Henry Irving (1838–1905) revived *Coriolanus* in 1901,[40] taking out significant scenes—the early fighting and Coriolanus's entry into Corioles alone—and modifying Volumnia's role. Not a physically commanding man, Irving, writes O'dell, produced a Coriolanus who was "transmuted from the heroic to the domestic and political arena, thereby becoming the history of Coriolanus in relations with his family and two rather antagonistic tribunes" (404–405). A revue in *The Antheneum* April 20, 1901, suggested the play moved to the "purely psychological" (405). "Neurotic and alienated outsider," writes Ripley, is what descriptions of Irving's character by reviewers suggest (195). Also, it appears that "Irving's Coriolanus took its inspiration not from the etherial splendor of high tragedy but the banalities of melodrama" (195), not exactly unusual during the period.

What was happening on American stages? In America, 1752 marks the beginning of a theater tradition with the emigration of Lewis Hallam and his London Company of Comedians. Edwin Forrest (1806–1872), the first native-born actor of repute, became popular in the 1820s. He did not play Coriolanus until January 10, 1838, at the Park Theater in New York, but he did continue to play the role until 1864. Like several well-known English tragedians, Forrest played the role many times, with at least forty performances. He traveled to England, and in 1860, played the role at Sadler's Wells in March and September, his only English tour for *Coriolanus*. Forrest was not the first to play Coriolanus in the states, though. Thomas Cooper, whose early years in London under the care of William Godwin left him well-versed in Shakespeare, began playing the role in 1799 and was his almost exclusively until Forrest began playing the part. Cooper modeled his style on Kemble's, and was regarded as a great classic actor during the years prior to Forrest's successes on the American Shakespearean stage (Shattuck 22–25). Forrest, too, modeled himself after Kemble (Berry, "Metamorphoses," 176). English actors Macready and Vandenhoff visited American shores and played the great Roman hero. Forrest performed the role in England. J. W. Wallack (1794–1864), between 1818 and 1824, played Coriolanus in both countries, the "first actor to commute regularly between England and the United States" (Ripley 213). On September 9, 1818, Wallack played Coriolanus at the Park Theater in New York, and on the first of January, 1821, he played Coriolanus at Drury Lane. His final performance of Coriolanus on January 2, 1846 at the Walnut Street Theater marked the end his playing the role, which he played at least eleven times. Although Wallack performed the tragic Roman in a number of respected theaters, it did not appear to be a role that fitted him well. His gestures and stage presence were attractive, but evidently Wallack lacked a speaking voice that was necessary for the role (Ripley 213).

The great productions of *Coriolanus* in the twentieth and twenty-first centuries have been British. In the 1970s, Ralph Berry claimed that Laurence Olivier's 1959 Stratford performance led by Peter Hall was the greatest Coriolanus performance of modern times. Olivier had played the part in 1938, too, but not to the acclaim he would later earn. The end of the play was visually moving. Being called "boy" by Aufidias, he "shrieks" the word "Boy," and in a rage, climbs steps. At the top, he throws away his sword. After shouting "I flutter'd your Volscians in Corioli," he is slain by swordsmen. Twelve feet above the stage, he falls forward, his ankles being grabbed by the surrounding Volscians, so that he dangles upside-down, dead (295), no longer a threat to Aufidias.

The last half of the twentieth century has had its share of great productions of *Coriolanus*. Two successful productions distinguished by their approaches to Shakespeare's text are worth mention and further study.

Terry Hand's 1977–1978 *Coriolanus* with Alan Howard as the Roman hero at Stratford-on-Avon was considered the most successful play of the season (Mulryne 323). Hand's setting and costumes alone remind us how far the hero has come from the "classic" theater Coriolanuses of the eighteenth, nineteenth, and early twentieth centuries and, at the same time, how close he seems to Shakespeare's. Hand's *Coriolanus* was presented on a set painted black, with sharp-edged "cliffs" on either side, also painted black, with metal faces. In contrast, the lights were "brilliant white," with a spotlight used to single out actors;[41] soldiers wore black leather, Coriolanus in close-fitted pants and vest with metal-studded trim. Metal boot buckles shone against the black of soldiers' boots.[42] Women wore loose tunics, the plebeians "jerkins" and hats.[43] The stage materials and costumes evoke for audiences a hard toughness that the hero elicits, a "robot designed by his mother for patrician conquest."[44] At the same time, an appearance of toughness draws attention to what it masks, a vulnerable, scarred human underneath, a man raised to fight and seek

Laurence Olivier in *Coriolanus*, SMT 1959. Photographer Angus McBean. © Royal Shakespeare Company. By Permission of the Shakespeare Birthplace Trust.

honor at great expense to any personal needs. Leather and metal, as clothing, are protective materials for the skin from pointed challenges to it, whether it be forces of nature or humanity.

Three months after the play's debut, J. R. Mulryne interviewed Howard on the role of Coriolanus. Howard, Mulryne noted, played the part with more "subtlety" than earlier actors who played up the arrogance and contempt of Coriolanus. As Howard pointed out, Coriolanus is a man who does what he says he will do. When he is asked to wear the gown of humility, he is embarrassed about it, says Howard; worse, Coriolanus shows that in this Rome, some "social forms weren't working, even as forms" (329). Another element that the actors playing noticed was how all the characters have an idea of what they want Coriolanus to be (326) yet another re-

Coriolanus, Royal Shakespeare Company 1977. Photographer Reg Wilson. © Royal Shakespeare Company. By Permission of the Shakespeare Birthplace Trust.

move from the actors who played the role presuming a proud, arrogant, virtuous Roman based more on old theatrical practices than on Shakespeare.

In *Coriolanus at the National*, author Kristina Bedford describes what she learned about Shakespearean-style acting on the set of Peter Hall's 1985 production of *Coriolanus* at London's National Theater. Hall's sensibility of how a Shakespearean play must be practiced and rehearsed by modern actors has led to successful productions. First, Hall says, actors must learn to speak in the Renaissance style, not collapse the rhetoric of Shakespeare into a naturalistic style of acting. Once Shakespeare's stylized language is mastered, then the actor can "build the role" by improvising. The text used by Hall was a "compilation" of the Arden edition of *Coriolanus* and the *First Folio* (Bedford, 25).

The setting, an amphitheater, had promenade seating on either side of a sandpit, a blend of Roman and modern. The gates of Rome stand at the center. Old posters reading "Vota DP" were hung, while iron scaffolding with danger signs posted complete the setting. The citizens and civilians were appareled in modern dress, the senate wore classical robes, the military figures wore futuristic styles, and the Roman women donned simple gowns. Aufidias and Coriolanus wore suits, but only loincloths when in battle. The tribunes wore suits under their cloaks. The working-class wore caps, jeans, and worn-out sweatshirts. During the citizen scenes, people in the audience were asked to "swell" the Roman crowds; different numbers were tried, and for practical reasons, fewer participants than planned swarmed the stage, but as Bedford points out, even the audience-participants sitting on the side emphasized the political arena of Coriolanus's Rome (41–43). Ian McClellan played Coriolanus, and after the run, Bedford interviewed him, asking him how he felt about Hall's approach to putting *Coriolanus* on stage. One of McClellan's responses was that he felt Hall emphasized the strengths of all the characters, an interesting view, considering the play has characters that seem to illuminate weaknesses (145).

The Royal Shakespeare Company's 2003 residency at the University of Michigan at Ann Arbor offered American audiences an opportunity to see the Royal Shakespeare Company perform *Coriolanus*. Cast with Greg Hicks as Coriolanus and Alison Fiske as Volumnia, the play managed to capture the Roman-ness of Coriolanus, a man who involved himself in the Roman community, mixing with patricians and plebeians alike. Coriolanus is not a solitary man—difficult, yes, but not aloof and indifferent. His banishment and alienation from his home, despite his obvious superiority to those who surround him, cause him pain, which he expresses in rage, desire for revenge, and even despair.

Hicks found in Coriolanus's verbal castigation of the plebeians a scathing wit. Rage, not pride, is what fed Coriolanus's desire to fight, to win, which Hicks exhibited. And if there were any questions about Shakespeare's sympathies to the plebeians, those are abated with concision. Coriolanus's rage is directed toward them most; his words are his weapons, and while they draw laughter from audience, the hatred inflicted upon the plebs should not be lost to the hatred inflicted upon himself. Coriolanus's bloody body, an open wound, is washed, then hidden. The rage that he feeds on brings him to ecstasy, but he cannot share that experience with the plebeians. Wounds close as does Coriolanus, who demands privacy, his body as his own, except when he wishes to give it to war, to Aufidias, to patricians, to those whom he sees as like him. This Coriolanus is an actor, somewhat campy, self-consciously theatrical, on the stage, articulate, razor sharp, vulnerable, playing the part his mother impressed upon him. Sadly, rage undoes Coriolanus.

Director David Farr saw in the 400 B.C. Roman Coriolanus a warrior's disposition to honor in his performance as a military figure, similar to the samurai of Japan's military aristocracy; thus, Hicks and fellow aristocratic cast members were costumed in Japanese apparel, and the accompanying music was eastern in texture. The stage was sparsely furnished. Lighting and pyrotechnics manipulated the visual focus of the audience. Smoke served the function of showing that a battle had taken place or as an entryway whence a character emerged. A departure from the severity of the stage was one in which the two tribunes were sitting at a small table, smugly dining and smoking, at the expense, no doubt, of the plebeians. Their decadent pleasures are soon ruined by the news that Coriolanus is returning to Rome with the Volscian army. A mincing Virgilia, much like the figure who appeared in early adaptations of *Coriolanus*, also showed the superficiality of the patrician class.[45] Volumnia was the powerful, dominating mother, bent on seeing her fantasy of glory and honor for her family exacted through her son. Hicks's Coriolanus, caught up in the idealism of honor to state and family, plays the part his mother designed for him[46] with, as one reviewer wrote of Hicks performance, "a sardonic view of heroism" (Liston 183). Perhaps not as Shakespeare would have regarded the Roman hero, but perhaps as modern audiences unfamiliar with Shakespeare's Romans prefer.

NOTES

1. Some have surmised that *Coriolanus* may have been written to be played before Inns of Court students at Blackfriars. Lee Bliss, ed., *Coriolanus* (Cambridge, England: Cambridge UP, 2000), p. 5.

2. Thomas G. Olsen, "Apolitical Shakespeare; or, the Restoration 'Coriolanus,'" *Studies in English Literature* 38 (1998), p. 422, thinks that Tate does more than domesticate the hero; "he domesticates Restoration political polemic and giv[es] it an affective, familial bias" by which "he makes broader claims for the inherently orderly and hierarchical stability of royal authority—a family, in effect, with Charles as the ultimate paterfamilias."

3. John Ripley, *Coriolanus on Stage in England and America, 1609–1994* (Madison, NJ: Fairleigh Dickinson UP, 1998), p. 55; McGugan's critical edition of Tate's adaptation includes more details of the publication.

4. Ruth McGugan, *Nahum Tate and the Coriolanus Tradition in English*

Drama with a Critical Edition of Tate's The Ingratitude of a Common-wealth (New York: Garland, 1987), p. 2.

5. Ibid., pp. 2–3.

6. Barbara A. Murray, *Restoration Shakespeare* (Madison, NJ: Fairleigh Dickinson UP, 2001), p. 182, claims that Tate also meant to make Coriolanus a more "consistent" hero as suggested by Horace in the *Art of Poetry*.

7. McGugan, *Nahum Tate*, p. 8.

8. Ripley, *Coriolanus on Stage*, thinks Mrs. Corey, who played "empty-headed society women," p. 69, might have played the part. What is evident is that dramatists were still writing plays with certain actors in mind.

9. McGugan, *Nahum Tate*, p. 21.

10. The near-rape of Virgilia would have appealed to the prurient interests of Restoration audiences. The advent of women actors on stage resulted in an interest in showing violence toward women: assaults, rapes, and blood-covered heroines were popular themes for audiences, says Elizabeth Howe in her book, *The First English Actresses: Women and Drama 1660–1700* (Cambridge, England: Cambridge UP, 1992), Chapter 2. Indeed, Nahum Tate was one of a few dramatists who adapted Shakespeare's plays by adding a "gratuitous rape." His adaptation of *Lear*, Howe relates, was "notorious" with its showing Cordelia being "seized by ruffians" and then being rescued by Edgar (p. 46).

11. Ripley, *Coriolanus on Stage*, p. 343.

12. Cited in ibid., p. 70.

13. John Dover Wilson, ed., *The Tragedy of Coriolanus* (Cambridge, England: Cambridge UP, 1960), p. xlii.

14. I am citing the Cornmarket Press facsimile of Dennis's work, which was published in 1720. Some pages have no page numbers. For instance, the prologue has no page numbering or signatures. The play also does not have line numbers. I will cite the page number where available, or the signature, if no page number is ascribed. If no signature exists, then I will simply describe the content as prologue, letter, and so on.

15. Dennis, it seems, felt that if Shakespeare had more classical training, he might have been an even better writer, says Harry Levin, "Critical Approaches to Shakespeare from 1660 to 1904," in *The Cambridge Companion to Shakespeare Studies*, ed. Stanley Wells (Cambridge, England: Cambridge UP, 1986), p. 216. He admired Shakespeare, to be sure, but the neoclassicism of his age led him to see Shakespeare through a narrow lens.

16. Dennis writes that "[b]efore this Play came upon the Stage, it had the Approbation of some of the very best Judges in *England*, who are so, and are universally acknowledg'd to be so, and who are too exalted both by their High Stations, and the Greatness of their Minds, to say a thing to me, which they did not think. I have had this Play long enough by me to form as true and as sure a Judgment of it my self, as any one can do, who understands Poetical Matters no better than my self" (A5V–A6R). Dennis evidently felt that he was a great dramatic poet.

17. Many presume Shakespeare hates the people; this is not a given. Hate is a strong word. As a patrician, Caius Martius shows his elitist bias toward the lower classes, but he intermingles with the people. True, he bullies them and "hates" their breaths, but that does not presume "hate."

18. Norman Rabkin, "Coriolanus: The Tragedy of Politics," *Shakespeare Quarterly* 17 (1966), pp. 197–98, acknowledges that by the next scene, it is no longer clear that the play can be read as a satire.

19. Wilson, *Tragedy*, pp. xliii–xliv.

20. McGugan, *Nahum Tate*, p. lxxxi.

21. Ibid., p. lxxxi.

22. From *The Works of James Thomson*, ed. Patrick Murdoch (London: John Dicks, 1874).

23. Ripley, *Coriolanus on Stage*, pp. 93–94.

24. Apparently, Quin's style, though popular, was "stiff and affected," writes Robert D. Hume, "Before the Bard: 'Shakespeare' in Early Eighteenth-Century London," *English Literary History* 64 (1997), p. 164.

25. Quin's image can be found at a number of places on the Internet.

26. Wilson, *Tragedy*, p. xliv.

27. *Bell's* used Garrick's promptbook for its edition of Shakespeare's *Coriolanus* (Ripley, *Coriolanus on Stage*, p. 109). Henry Mossop played Caius Martius, and while the eight-day run was successful, Ripley, p. 114, tells us that Shakespeare's "unadulterated text" would not be staged for about seventy-five years.

28. Wilson, *Tragedy*, p. xliv.

29. From the facsimile of the 1755 edition of Thomas Sheridan's *Coriolanus or The Roman Matron*, (Cornmarket Press, 1969), pp. 46–47. Compare this passage with Thomson's, in which an officer brings news to Tullus Aufidias of a visitor:

> My Lord,
> One of exalted port, his visage hid,
> Has plac'd himself upon your sacred hearth,
> Beneath the dread protection of your Lares;
> And sits majestic there in solemn silence. (*Coriolanus* 1.3.5–8)

from James Thomson, *The Works of James Thomson*, ed. Patrick Murdoch (London: John Dicks, 1874).

30. Ripley, *Coriolanus on Stage*, p. 106.

31. Esther K. Sheldon, "Sheridan's *Coriolanus*: An 18th-Century Compromise," *Shakespeare Quarterly* 14 (1963), p. 161.

32. Qtd. in Ralph Berry, "The Metamorphoses of *Coriolanus*," *Shakespeare Quarterly* 26 (1975), p. 174.

33. George Odell, *Shakespeare from Betterton to Irving*, 2 vols. (New York: Benjamin Blom, 1920), 2:104.

34. Ibid., 2:87.

35. Tracy Davis, "'Reading Shakespeare by Flashes of Lightening': Challenging the Foundations of Romantic Acting Theory," *English Literary History* 62 (1995), p. 933.

36. Berry, "Metamorphoses," 180.

37. Odell cites *John Bull*, March 19, 1838, on Macready's Covent Garden performance (2:211–13).

38. Odell cites *The Times*, April 16, 1901 (2:456).

39. Ripley, *Coriolanus on Stage*, p. 199.

40. This was Irving's last stage performance, says Berry, "Metamorphoses," p. 177.

41. J.R. Mulryne, "*Coriolanus* at Stratford-on-Avon: Three Interviews," *Shakespeare Quarterly* 29 (1978), p. 323.

42. Ripley, *Coriolanus on Stage*, p. 321.

43. Mulryne, "*Coriolanus* at Stratford-on-Avon," p. 323.

44. Ripley, *Coriolanus on Stage*, p. 323.

45. I saw this performance on March 8, 2003, in Ann Arbor, Michigan. Hosted by the University of Michigan, the Royal Shakespeare Company performed *The Merry Wives* as well.

46. William T. Liston's review, in "*Coriolanus* and *The Merry Wives of Windsor*: The Royal Shakespeare Company at the University of Michigan, Ann Arbor, Michigan, 1–2 March 2003," *Theatre Journal* 55.4 (2003), 725–726 of the performance:

> *Coriolanus*, directed by David Farr, was costumed as if set in the Samurai era of Japan. Three warriors were seated on low stools at the rear of the stage with their backs to the audience oblivious to the opening scene of rioting citizens including several women. A red circle on the floor often contained the action and defined who was in and out. This production distinguished simply and clearly the various factions in Rome. A copper-toned semi-circular back wall signified stone or marble thereby emphasizing the lack of softness and humanity. Guns and cigarettes blurred any real sense of medieval Japan or ancient Rome. However, the Japanese costuming suggested ritual violence, especially in the stylized movement of the stiff trousers of Coriolanus.
>
> Greg Hicks proved himself a natural Coriolanus as he displayed contempt for commoners and impatience with fools. As he emerged bathed in Volscian blood from the gates of Corioles, he palpably loathed his own soldiers as they gloated over their pillage. His later attempt to court the favor of the stinking crowd with a smile, while wearing the tattered gown of humility, ended predictably in exasperation. Richard Cordery gives an impressive performance as Menenius, whose equally contemptuous taunting of the Tribunes underscored Coriolanus's arrogance after his last victory: "Mar-tius has more cause to be proud." (2.1.145–46)
>
> Alison Fiske played Volumnia with an iron voice and a similar mien. Hannah Young attained the "gracious silence" (2.1.175) of Virgilia, Coriolanus's

wife, with a robust emotional life. Director Farr included her in act 3 scene 2 and had her run offstage in tears as Coriolanus declared "I will not do't" (3.2.120) in response to the appeals of Volumnia and Cominius to humble himself for popular votes. Claire Carrie presented Valeria as a silly woman in her manner and even in her walk, sashaying her derriere in her first appearance.

The first act ended with Coriolanus's trial for tyranny, during which two women, kneeling at the back of the red circle briskly recorded the conduct of the event on typewriters. As the banished Coriolanus exited between the two typists, he signaled them to resume their note taking on "There's a world elsewhere." (3.3.135)

In the second act, Coriolanus, in a stylized combat scene, quickly disposed of a challenge by a servant of Aufidius (Chuk Iwuji), who soon had him in a semi-erotic embrace. When Volumnia came to plead with her son to spare Rome, Aufidius sat impassively at the rear of the set, hearing everything, yet revealing no sign that he heard or thought anything.

As the rival warriors confronted each other for the final battle and Coriolanus was about to strike the first blow with his sword, a nameless Volscian soldier shot him in the back. Coriolanus fell, rose with difficulty, and as he again raised his sword for the attack, he was shot in the back a second time and fell yet again. The mob immediately piled on to complete the desecration, which was signified when one of the assassins held Coriolanus's heart aloft. (725–26)

SELECTED BIBLIOGRAPHY

BIOGRAPHY

Honan, Park. 1998. *Shakespeare: A Life*. Oxford: Oxford UP.

Humes, James C. 1993. *Citizen Shakespeare: A Social and Political Portrait*. Westport, CT: Praeger.

Jones, Emrys. 1977. *The Origins of Shakespeare*. Oxford: Oxford UP.

Schoenbaum, Samuel. 1991. *Shakespeare's Lives*. New York: Oxford UP.

PRIMARY TEXTS AND ADAPTATIONS

Dennis, John. [1720] 1969. *The Invader of his Country; or The Fatal Resentment*. London: Cornmarket P.

Grass, Günter. 1967. *The Plebeians Rehearse the Uprising*. Trans. Ralph Manheim. London: Secker and Warburg.

Kökeritz, Helge. 1954. *Mr. William Shakespeare's Comedies, Histories, & Tragedies: A Facsimile Edition*. New Haven, CT: Yale UP.

North, Thomas. 1929. *Plutarch's Lives of Noble Grecians and Romanes, 1579*. 5 vols. London: Nonesuch P.

Sheridan, Thomas. [1755] 1969. *Coriolanus, or The Roman Matron*. Facsimile. London: Cornmarket P.

Tate, Nahum. 1987. *Nahum Tate and the Coriolanus Tradition in English Drama with a Critical Edition of Tate's The Ingratitude of a Common-wealth*. New York: Garland.

Thomson, James. 1874. *Coriolanus. The Works of James Thomson*. London: John Dicks.

TEXT AND SOURCES ON SHAKESPEARE

Baldwin, T. W. 1927. *The Organization and Personnel of the Shakespearn Company*. Princeton, NJ: Princeton UP, 1927.

Bowers, Fredson. 1955. *On Editing Shakespeare and the Elizabethan Dramatists*. Philadelphia: U of Pennsylvania P.

Brooke, C. F. Tucker, ed. 1909. *Shakespeare's Plutarch*. 2 vols. London: Chatto and Windus.

Bullough, Geoffrey, ed. 1964. *Narrative and Dramatic Sources of Shakespeare, V: The Roman Plays*. London: Routledge.

Chambers, E. K. 1930. *William Shakespeare: The Elizabethan Stage*. 4 vols. Oxford: Clarendon, Vol 3.

Greg, W. W. 1955. *The Shakespeare First* Folio: *Its Bibliographical and Textual History*. Oxford: Clarendon.

Hinman, Charleton. 1963. *The Printing and Proofreading of the First* Folio *of Shakespeare*. 2 vols. Oxford: Clarendon, Vol. 1 and Vol 2.

Honigman, E.A.J. 1965. *The Stability of Shakespeare's Text*. London: Edward Arnold.

Lounsbury, Thomas R. [1906] 1974. *The First Editors of Shakespeare: Pope and Theobald*. Folcraft, PA: Folcraft Library Editions.

Muir, Kenneth. 1957. *Shakespeare's Sources I: Comedies and Tragedies*. London: Methuen and Company.

EDITIONS

Bliss, Lee, ed. 2000. *Coriolanus*. Cambridge, England: Cambridge UP.

Brockbank, Philip, ed. 1976. *Coriolanus*. The Arden Shakespeare. London: Methuen.

Parker, R. B., ed. 1994. *Coriolanus*. New York: Oxford UP.

GENERAL CRITICISM ON SHAKESPEARE'S TRAGEDIES

Adelman, Janet. 1992. *Suffocating Mothers: Fantasies of Maternal Origin in Shakespeare's Plays, Hamlet to The Tempest*. New York: Routledge.

Bradley, A. C. [1904] 1960. *Shakespearean Tragedy*. London: Macmillan.

Bratchel, D. F., ed. 1990. *Shakespearean Tragedy*. New York: Routledge.

Cohen, Walter. 1990. "Political Criticism of Shakespeare." *Shakespeare Reproduced: The Text in History & Ideology*. Ed. Jean E. Howard and Marion F. O'Connor. New York: Routledge.

Dollimore, Jonathan. 1984. *Radical Tragedy: Religion, Ideology and Power in the Drama of Shakespeare and His Contemporaries*. London: Routledge.

French, Marilyn. 1981. *Shakespeare's Division of Experience*. New York: Summit Books, 265–76.

Greenblatt, Stephen. 1980. *Renaissance Self-Fashioning: From More to Shakespeare*. Chicago: U of Chicago P.

Kahn, Coppélia. 1997. *Roman Shakespeare: Warriors, Wounds, and Women*. New York: Routledge.

Kiernan, Victor. 1996. *Eight Tragedies of Shakespeare: A Marxist Study*. London: Verso.

Knight, G. Wilson. 1965. *The Imperial Theme*. London: Methuen.

Mack, Maynard. 1996. "The Jacobean Shakespeare: Some Observations on the Construction of the Tragedies." *Shakespeare's Late Tragedies: A Collection of Critical Essays*. Ed. Susan L. Wofford. New York: Prentice-Hall, 22–45.

Patterson, Annabel. 1989. *Shakespeare and the Popular Voice*. Oxford: Blackwell.

Platt, Michael. 1983. *Rome and Romans According to Shakespeare*. New York: University Press of America.

Stirling, Brents. 1949. *The Populace in Shakespeare*. New York: Columbia UP.

Wells, Robin Headlam. 1986. *Shakespeare: Politics and State*. London: Macmillan.

CRITICISM ON CORIOLANUS

Barton, Anne. 1985. "Livy, Machiavelli, and Shakespeare's Coriolanus." *Shakespeare Survey* 38: 115–29.

Bedford, Kristina. 1992. *Coriolanus at the National: "Th'Interpretation of the Time."* London: Associated UP.

Bliss, Lee. 1999. *"What Hath a Quarter-Century of* Coriolanus *Criticism Wrought?" The Shakespearean International Yearbook, II: Where Are We Now in Shakespearean Studies?* Ed. W. R. Elton and John M. Mucciolo. Aldershot, England: Ashgate, 63–75.

Bradley, A. C. 1912. "Coriolanus." *The Annual Shakespeare Lectures*. New York: Oxford UP.

Bristol, Michael D. 1987. "Lenten Butchery: Legitimation Crisis in Coriolanus." *Shakespeare Reproduced: The Text in History and Ideology*. Ed. Jean E. Howard and Marion F. O'Connor. New York: Methuen.

Calderwood, James L. 1966. "*Coriolanus*: Wordless Meanings and Meaningless Words." *Studies in English Literature* 6: 211–24.

Cavell, Stanley. 1983. "Who Does the Wolf Love?: Reading Coriolanus." *Representations* 3: 1–20.

Charney, Maurice. 1956. "The Dramatic Use of Imagery in Shakespeare's Coriolanus." *English Literary History* 23: 183–93.

Christensen, Ann C. 1997. "The Return of the Domestic in *Coriolanus*." *Studies in English Literature* 37: 295–316.

Goldberg, Jonathan. 2000. "The Anus in Coriolanus." *Historicism, Psycho-*

analysis, and Early Modern Culture. Ed. and intro. Carla Mazzio and Douglas Trevor. New York: Routledge, 260–71.

Granville-Barker, Harley. 1946. *Prefaces to Shakespeare: Antony and Cleopatra and Coriolanus*. Princeton, NJ: Princeton UP.

Gurr, Andrew. 1975. "Coriolanus and the Body Politic." *Shakespeare Survey* 28: 63–69.

Hale, David. 1971. "The Death of a Political Metaphor." *Shakespeare Quarterly* 22: 197–202.

Halio, Jay. 1970. "*Coriolanus*. Shakespeare's Drama of Reconciliation." *Shakespeare Studies* 6: 289–303.

Huffman, Clifford Chalmers. 1971. Coriolanus *in Context*. Lewisburg, PA: Bucknell UP.

Hunt, Maurice. 1991. " 'Violent'st' Complementary: The Double Warriors of Coriolanus." *Studies in English Literature* 31: 309–25.

Jagendorf, Zvi. 1990. "Coriolanus: Body Politic and Private Parts." *Shakespeare Quarterly* 41: 455–69.

Miola, Robert. 1983. *Shakespeare's Rome*. Cambridge, England: Cambridge UP.

Poole, Adrian. 1988. *Coriolanus. Twayne's New Critical Introductions to Shakespeare*. Boston: Twayne Publishers.

Rabkin, Norman. 1966. "Coriolanus: The Tragedy of Politics." *Shakespeare Quarterly* 17: 195–212.

THEATER

Davis, Tracy. 1995. " 'Reading Shakespeare by Flashes of Lightening': Challenging the Foundations of Romantic Acting Theory." *English Literary History* 62: 933–54.

Gurr, Andrew. 1992. *The Shakespearean Stage 1574–1642*. 3rd ed. Cambridge, England: Cambridge UP.

Odell, George. [1920] 1963. *Shakespeare From Betterton to Irving*. 2 vols. New York: Benjamin Blom.

Ripley, John. 1998. *Coriolanus on Stage in England and America, 1609–1994*. Madison, NJ: Fairleigh Dickinson UP.

Wickham, Glynn, et al. 2000. *Theatre in Europe: A Documentary History: English Professional Theatre, 1530–1660*. Cambridge, England: Cambridge UP.

WORKS CITED

Adelman, Janet. 1992. *Suffocating Mothers: Fantasies of Maternal Origin in Shakespeare's Plays, Hamlet to The Tempest.* New York: Routledge.

Aristotle. 1996. *Poetics.* Trans. and ed. Malcolm Heath. New York: Penguin.

Aubrey, Karen. 1996. "Shifting Masks, Roles, and Satiric Personae: Suggestions for Exploring the Edge of Genre in *Coriolanus.*" Coriolanus: *Critical Essays.* Ed. David Wheeler. New York: Garland, 299–338.

Baldwin, T. W. 1927. *The Organization and Personnel of the Shakespearean Company.* Princeton, NJ: Princeton UP.

Barton, Anne. 1985. "Livy, Machiavelli, and Shakespeare's Coriolanus." *Shakespeare Survey* 38: 115–29.

Bedford, Kristina. 1992. *Coriolanus at the National: "Th'Interpretation of the Time."* London: Associated UP.

Berry, Ralph. 1975. "The Metamorphoses of *Coriolanus.*" *Shakespeare Quarterly* 26: 172–85.

———. 1973. "Sexual Imagery in *Coriolanus.*" *Studies in English Literature* 13: 301–16.

———. 1988. *Shakespeare and Social Class.* Atlantic Highlands, NJ: Humanities Press International.

Bliss, Lee, ed. 2000. *Coriolanus.* Cambridge, England: Cambridge UP.

Bowers, Fredson. 1955. *On Editing Shakespeare and the Elizabethan Dramatists.* Philadelphia: U of Pennsylvania P.

Bradley, A. C. 1912. "Coriolanus." *The Annual Shakespeare Lectures.* New York: Oxford UP, American Branch.

———. [1904] 1960. *Shakespearean Tragedy.* London: Macmillan.

Bratchell, D. F., ed. 1990. *Shakespearean Tragedy.* New York: Routledge.

Bristol, Michael D. 1987. "Lenten Butchery: Legitimation Crisis in Coriolanus."

Shakespeare Reproduced: The Text in History and Ideology. Ed. Jean E. Howard and Marion F. O'Connor. New York: Methuen.

Brockbank, Philip, ed. 1976. *Coriolanus. The Arden Shakespeare*. London: Methuen.

Budra, Paul. 2000. *A Mirror for Magistrates and the de casibus Tradition*. Toronto: U of Toronto P.

Bullough, Geoffrey, ed. 1964. *Narrative and Dramatic Sources of Shakespeare, V: The Roman Plays*. 8 vols. London: Routledge.

Calderwood, James L. 1966. "*Coriolanus*: Wordless Meanings and Meaningless Words." *Studies in English Literature* 6: 211–24.

Campbell, Lily B. 1952. *Shakespeare's Tragic Heroes*. New York: Barnes and Noble.

Campbell, Oscar James. 1943. *Shakespeare's Satire*. New York: Oxford UP.

Cantor, Paul A. 1976. *Shakespeare's Rome, Republic and Empire*. Ithaca: Cornell UP.

Cavell, Stanley. 1983. "Who Does the Wolf Love?: Reading Coriolanus." *Representations* 3: 1–20.

Cefalu, Paul. 2000. " 'The End of Absolutism': Shakespeare's *Coriolanus* and the Consensual Nature of the Early Modern State." *Renaissance Forum* 4: 34 paragraphs.

Chambers, E. K. 1930. *William Shakespeare: The Elizabethan Stage*. 4 vols. Oxford: Clarendon, vol. 3.

Charney, Maurice. 1956. "The Dramatic Use of Imagery in Shakespeare's Coriolanus." *English Literary History* 23: 183–93.

Christensen, Ann C. 1997. "The Return of the Domestic in *Coriolanus*." *Studies in English Literature* 37: 295–316.

Cohen, Walter. 1990. "Political Criticism of Shakespeare." *Shakespeare Reproduced: The Text in History & Ideology*. Ed. Jean E. Howard and Marion F. O'Connor. New York: Routledge.

Davidson, Clifford. 1968. "*Coriolanus*: A Study in Political Dislocation." *Shakespeare Studies* 4: 263–74.

Davis, Tracy. 1995. " 'Reading Shakespeare by Flashes of Lightening': Challenging the Foundations of Romantic Acting Theory." *English Literary History* 62: 933–54.

Dennis, John. [1720] 1969. *The Invader of his Country; or The Fatal Resentment*. London: Cornmarket P.

Dollimore, Jonathan. 1984. *Radical Tragedy: Religion, Ideology and Power in the Drama of Shakespeare and His Contemporaries*. London: Routledge.

Evans, G. Blakemore. 1997. The Riverside Shakespeare. 2nd edition. Boston: Houghton Mifflin.

French, Marilyn. 1981. *Shakespeare's Division of Experience*. New York: Summit Books, 265–76.

Frye Dean. 1965. "Commentary in Shakespeare: The Case of *Coriolanus*." *Shakespeare Studies* 1: 105–17.

Garganigo, Alex. 2002. "*Coriolanus*, the Union Controversy, and Access to the Royal Person." *Studies in English Literature* 42: 335–59.

Goldman, Michael. 1981. "Characterizing Coriolanus." *Shakespeare Survey* 34: 73–84.

Granville-Barker, Harley. 1946. *Prefaces to Shakespeare*: Antony and Cleopatra *and* Coriolanus. Princeton, NJ: Princeton UP.

Grass, Günter. 1967. *The Plebeians Rehearse the Uprising*. Trans. Ralph Manheim. London: Secker and Warburg.

Great Britain Public Record Office. 1967. *Calendar of State Papers, Domestic Series, of the Reigns of Edward VI, Mary, Elizabeth [and James I] 1547–1625*. 12 vols. Ed. Robert Lemon. Nendeln, Liechtenstein: Kraus Reprint.

Greenblatt, Stephen. *Renaissance Self Fashioning: From More to Shakespeare*. Chicago: U of Chicago P, 1980.

Greg, W. W. 1955. *The Shakespeare First Folio: Its Bibliographical and Textual History*. Oxford: Clarendon Press.

Gurr, Andrew. 1975. "Coriolanus and the Body Politic." *Shakespeare Survey* 28: 63–69.

———. 1992. *The Shakespearean Stage*. 3rd ed. Cambridge, England: Cambridge UP.

Hale, David. 1971. "The Death of a Political Metaphor." *Shakespeare Quarterly* 22: 197–202.

Halio, Jay. 1970. "*Coriolanus*. Shakespeare's Drama of Reconciliation." *Shakespeare Studies* 6: 289–303.

Hampton, Timothy. Writing History: The Rhetoric of Exemplarity in Renaissance Literature. Ithaca: Cornell UP, 1990.

Hinman, Charleton. 1963. *The Printing and Proofreading of the First Folio of Shakespeare*. 2 vols. Oxford: Clarendon, Vol. 1 and Vol. 2.

Holstun, James. 1983. "Tragic Superfluity in Coriolanus." *English Literary History* 50: 485–507.

Honan, Park. 1998. *Shakespeare: A Life*. Oxford: Oxford UP.

Honigman, E.A.J. 1965. *The Stability of Shakespeare's Text*. London: Edward Arnold.

Howe, Elizabeth. 1992. *The First English Actresses: Women and Drama 1660–1700*. Cambridge, England: Cambridge UP.

Hume, Robert D. 1997. "Before the Bard: 'Shakespeare' in Early Eighteenth-Century London." *English Literary History* 64: 41–75.

Hunt, Maurice. 1991. " 'Violent'st' Complementary: The Double Warriors of Coriolanus." *Studies in English Literature* 31: 309–25.

Iser, Wolfgang. 1993. *Staging Politics: The Lasting Impact of Shakespeare's Histories*. Trans. David Henry Wilson. New York: Columbia UP.

Jagendorf, Zvi. 1990. "Coriolanus: Body Politic and Private Parts." *Shakespeare Quarterly* 41: 455–69.

Jones, Emrys. 1977. *The Origins of Shakespeare.* Oxford: Oxford UP.

Jonson, Ben. 1981. *Sejanus, His Fall in Ben Jonson: Five Plays*. Ed. and intro. G. A. Wilkes. Oxford: Oxford UP.

Jorgenson, Paul A. 1949. "Shakespeare's Coriolanus: Elizabethan Soldier." *PMLA* 64: 221–35.

Kahn, Coppélia. 1997. *Roman Shakespeare: Warriors, Wounds, and Women*. New York: Routledge.

Knight, G. Wilson. 1965. *The Imperial Theme*. London: Methuen.

Knowles, Ronald. 2002. *Shakespeare's Arguments with History*. New York: Palgrave.

Kökeritz, Helge, ed. [1623] 1954. *Mr. William Shakespeare's Comedies, Histories, & Tragedies: A Facsimile Edition*. New Haven, CT: Yale UP.

Kujawinska-Courtney, Krystyna. 1993. *"Interpretation of the Time": The Dramaturgy of Shakespeare's Roman Plays*. Victoria, BC: University of Victoria P.

Leggatt, Alexander. 1988. *Shakespeare's Political Drama: The History Plays and the Roman Plays*. New York: Routledge.

Levin, Harry. 1986. "Critical Approaches to Shakespeare from 1660 to 1904." *The Cambridge Companion to Shakespeare Studies*. Ed. Stanley Wells. Cambridge, England: Cambridge UP, 213–29.

Liston, William T. 2003. "*Coriolanus* and *The Merry Wives of Windsor*: The Royal Shakespeare Company at the University of Michigan, Ann Arbor, Michigan. 1–2 March 2003." *Theatre Journal* 55.4: 725–26.

Lounsbury, Thomas R. [1906] 1974. *The First Editors of Shakespeare: Pope and Theobald*. Folcraft, PA: Folcraft Library Editions.

MacCallum, M. W. 1910. *Shakespeare's Roman Plays and Their Background*. London: Macmillan. Rpt. London: Macmillan, 1935.

Mack, Maynard. 1996. "The Jacobean Shakespeare: Some Observations on the Construction of the Tragedies." *Shakespeare's Late Tragedies: A Collection of Critical Essays*. Ed. Susan L. Wofford. New York: Prentice-Hall, 22–45.

Macready, William Charles. [1912] 1969. *The Diaries of William Charles Macready, 1833–1851*. 2 vols. Ed. William Toynbee. Vol. 1. New York: Benjamin Blom.

Marcus, Leah S. 1996. "*Coriolanus* and the Expansion of City Liberties." *Shakespeare's Late Tragedies: A Collection of Critical Essays*. Ed. Susan L. Wofford. New York: Prentice-Hall, 188–96.

McGugan, Ruth. 1987. *Nahum Tate and the Coriolanus Tradition in English Drama with a Critical Edition of Tate's The Ingratitude of a Commonwealth.* New York: Garland.

McKenzie, Stanley D. 1986. " 'Unshout the Noise That Banish'd Martius': Structural Paradox and Dissembling in Coriolanus." *Shakespeare Studies* 18: 189–204.

McKerrow, Ronald B. 1939. *The Treatment of Shakespeare's Text by His Earlier Editors: 1709–1768*. Folcraft, PA: Folcraft Press.

Meszaros, Patricia K. 1976. " 'There Is a World Elsewhere': Tragedy and History in *Coriolanus*." *Studies in English Literature* 16: 273–85.

Miller, Shannon. 1992. "Topicality and Subversion in William Shakespeare's Coriolanus." *Studies in English Language* 32: 287–310.

Miola, Robert. 1983. *Shakespeare's Rome*. Cambridge, England: Cambridge UP.

Mitchell, Charles. 1965. "Coriolanus: Power as Honor." *Shakespeare Studies* 1: 199–226.

Monk, Samuel Holt, intro. 1948. "Some Account of the Life of Mr. William Shakespear (1709) by Nicholas Rowe." *The Augustan Reprint Society Publications* 17: 1–11. Rpt. by Kraus Reprint Society, 1967.

Mulryne, J.R. 1978. "*Coriolanus* at Stratford-on-Avon: Three Interviews." *Shakespeare Quarterly* 29: 323–32.

Murray, Barbara A. 2001. *Restoration Shakespeare*. Madison, NJ: Fairleigh Dickinson.

Odell, George. [1920] 1963. *Shakespeare from Betterton to Irving*. 2 vols. New York: Benjamin Blom.

Oliver, H.J. 1959. "Coriolanus as Tragic Hero." *Shakespeare Quarterly* 10: 53–60.

Olsen, Thomas G. 1998. "Apolitical Shakespeare; or, the Restoration 'Coriolanus.' " *Studies in English Literature* 38: 411–25.

Palmer, John. 1961. *Political Characters of Shakespeare*. London: Macmillan.

Paris, Bernard J. 1991. *Character as a Subversive Force in Shakespeare: The History and Roman Plays*. London: Associated UP.

Paster, Gail Kern. 1985. *The Idea of the City in the Age of Shakespeare*. Athens: U of Georgia P.

Patterson, Anabelle. 1989. *Shakespeare and the Popular Voice*. New York: Blackwell.

Pettet, E.C. 1950. "Coriolanus and the Midlands Insurrection of 1607." *Shakespeare Survey* 3: 34–42.

Plotz, John. 1996. "*Coriolanus* and the Failure of Performatives." *English Literary History* 63: 809–32.

Rabkin, Norman. 1966. "Coriolanus: The Tragedy of Politics." *Shakespeare Quarterly* 17: 195–212.

Rackin, Phyllis. 1978. *Shakespeare's Tragedies*. New York: Frederick Ungar.

Reynolds, Bryan. 2000. " 'What is the city but the people?': Transversal Performance and Radical Politics in Shakespeare's Coriolanus and Brecht's Coriolan." *Shakespeare Without Class*. Ed. Donald Hedrick and Bryan Reynolds. New York: Palgrave.

Ripley, John. 1998. *Coriolanus on Stage in England and America, 1609–1994*. Madison, NJ: Fairleigh Dickinson UP.

Riss, Arthur. 1992. "The Belly Politic: Coriolanus and the Revolt of Language." *English Literary History* 59: 53–75.

Ronan, Clifford. 1995. *Antike Roman: Power Symbology and the Roman Play in Early Modern England, 1585–1635*. Athens: U of Georgia P.

Schoenbaum, S. 1979. *Shakespeare, The Globe, and the World*. Oxford: Oxford UP.

Seary, Peter. 1990. *Lewis Theobald and the Editing of Shakespeare*. Oxford: Clarendon P.

Sen, Sailendra Kumar. 1958. "What Happens in *Coriolanus*." *Shakespeare Quarterly* 9: 331–45.

Shattuck, Charles H. 1976. *Shakespeare on the American Stage: From the Hallams to Edwin Booth*. Washington DC: Folger Shakespeare Library.

Sheldon, Esther K. 1963. "Sheridan's *Coriolanus*: An 18th-Century Compromise." *Shakespeare Quarterly* 14: 153–61.

Sheridan, Thomas. [1755] 1969. *Coriolanus, or The Roman Matron*. Facsimile. London: Cornmarket P.

Sicherman, Carol M. 1972. "Coriolanus: The Failure of Words." *English Literary History* 39: 189–207.

Sidney, Philip. 1966. *A Defense of Poetry*. Ed. J. A. Van Dorsten. Oxford: Oxford UP.

Siegel, Paul N. 1986. *Shakespeare's English and Roman History Plays: A Marxist Approach*. Rutherford, NJ: Fairleigh Dickinson UP.

Smirnov, A. A. 1970. *Shakespeare: A Marxist Interpretation*. Trans. Sonia Volochova for *The Critics Group Series*, no. 2 (1936), 76–78. Rpt. in *Twentieth Century Interpretations of* Coriolanus. Ed. James E. Phillips. Englewood Cliffs, NJ: Prentice Hall, 105–107.

Sorge, Thomas. 1987. "The Failure of Orthodoxy in Coriolanus." *Shakespeare Reproduced: The Text in History and Ideology*. Ed. Jean E. Howard and Marion F. O'Connor. New York: Methuen.

Sprengnether, Madelon. 1995. "Annihilating Intimacy in *Coriolanus*." *Coriolanus: Critical Essays*. Ed. David Wheeler. New York: Garland.

Thomas, Vivian. 1989. *Shakespeare's Roman Worlds*. London: Routledge.

Thomson, James. 1874. *Coriolanus. The Works of James Thomson*, ed. Patrick Murdoch. London: John Dicks.

Tillyard, E. M.W. 1944. *The Elizabethan World Picture*. New York: Vintage Books.

Tolman, Albert H. 1922. "The Structure of Shakespeare's Tragedies with Special Reference to Coriolanus." *Modern Language Notes* 37: 449–58.

Traversi, D. A. 1956. *An Approach to Shakespeare*. Garden City, NY: Doubleday.

———. 1963. *The Roman Plays*. Stanford, CA: Stanford UP.

Walker, Roy. 1951. "The Northern Star: An Essay on the Roman Plays." *Shakespeare Quarterly* 4: 287–93.

Webster, Graham. 1999. *The Roman Invasion of Britain*. New York: Routledge.

Wells, Charles. 1994. *The Wide Arch*. New York: St. Martin's.

Wells, Robin Headlam. 1986. *Shakespeare, Politics, and the State*. London: Macmillan.

Wheeler, Richard P. 1980. "'Since first we were dissevered': Trust and Autonomy in Shakespearean Tragedy and Romance." *Representing Shakespeare: New Psychoanalytic Essays*. Ed. Murray M. Schwartz and Coppélia Kahn. Baltimore: Johns Hopkins UP, 150–69.

Wickham, Glynn, et. al. 2000. *Theatre in Europe: A Documentary History: English Professional Theatre, 1530–1660*. Cambridge, England: Cambridge UP.

Wilson, Emmett, Jr. 1995. "Coriolanus: The Anxious Bridegroom." *Coriolanus: Critical Essays*. Ed. David Wheeler. New York: Garland, 93–110.

Wilson, J. Dover. 1956. "The New Way with Shakespeare's Texts: An Introduction for Lay Readers." *Shakespeare Survey* 9: 69–80.

Wilson, John Dover, ed. 1960. *The Tragedy of Coriolanus*. Cambridge, England: Cambridge UP.

INDEX

About the Author

MARY STEIBLE is an assistant professor at Purdue University North Central. Her current projects include a paper on Shakespeare's concept of civil liberties as presented in *Coriolanus* and a longer effort on Shakespeare's Roman matrons as authoritative community voices in their respective texts.